RETURN TO BIG GRASS

RETURN TO BIG GRASS

Ducks Unlimited
Leader in Wetlands
Conservation

Richard Wentz, *Editor*
Nicoletta Barrie, *Managing Editor*
Richard Wentz, Nicoletta Barrie, Mike Beno,
George Stanley, Richard S. Grozik, James Dudas, *Writers*
Richard Fish, *Illustrator*

Published by
Ducks Unlimited, Inc.
Hazard K. Campbell, *President*
Peter H. Coors, *Chairman of the Board*
Robert M. Eberhardt, *Executive Committee Chairman*
Dale E. Whitesell, *Executive Vice President*
Stanley W. Koenig, Sr., *Secretary, 50th Anniversary Chairman*
William M. Rue, *Treasurer*
Kenneth V. McCreary, *Executive Secretary*

Ducks Unlimited, Inc.
One Waterfowl Way
Long Grove, Illinois 60047

This book is dedicated to the volunteers of Ducks Unlimited, Inc.

Ducks Unlimited, Inc., is a private, nonprofit organization which
conserves wetland habitat for waterfowl and other wildlife. DU
was incorporated by a group of farsighted conservationists on
January 29, 1937.

Library of Congress Cataloging in Publication Data
Ducks Unlimited, Inc.
Return to Big Grass
86-050813

ISBN 0-9617279-0-X

Cover painting by Francis Lee Jaques
Design by Paul Nelson, Mobium Corporation for Design and Communication
Composition by Design Typographers, Inc.
Printed by Graphic Arts Center, Portland, Oregon

ACKNOWLEDGMENTS

The editors wish to extend their appreciation to D. Stewart Morrison, Executive Vice President of Ducks Unlimited Canada and Dr. Eric W. Gustafson, Executive Vice President of Ducks Unlimited de Mexico, who cooperated graciously when the help of members of their staffs was needed in the gathering of research material for this book. Personnel include: Dr. A. J. Macaulay, T. K. Slater, T. G. Neraasen, A. S. Glover, Keith McAloney, John Wile, Gary Garrioch, Lawrence Kelly, Rick Andrews, Dave Clayton, Clem Jones, Chris Smith, David Klassen and Don Fiddler, all of DU Canada; and Emilio Rangel-Woodyard and Federico Kleen of Ducks Unlimited de Mexico.

Special thanks to the James Ford Bell Museum of Natural History, University of Minnesota in Minneapolis, for permission to feature Francis Lee Jaques' oil painting *The Old West Passes* as both a trade edition cover and limited-edition print accompanying the deluxe limited edition of this book. Thanks, as well, to all DU Artists of the Year, free-lance writer John Madson for his Foreword, the late Jimmy Robinson of *Sports Afield*, Jack Barrie and Bob Gass of the Royal Canadian Mounted Police, Bill Webster of Wild Wings, Inc., Bob Uchtmann of the Manitoba Department of Natural Resources, trappers Phil Reader, Norman Jeb and Edwin Jeb of The Pas, Manitoba, Harold Wells of The Pas and Dave Phillips of the Saskatchewan Department of Parks and Renewable Resources.

CONTENTS

FOREWORD

About 25 years ago, with an ancient bellhop named Bobo bringing me pots of coffee, I finally managed to hack out the final passages in a little book called *The Mallard*. It was at the old Riceland Hotel in Stuttgart, Arkansas, where I was dividing my days between a portable typewriter and the flooded oak timber of Winchester's Greenbrier Club. Writing is never easy, and the onerous chore wasn't made any lighter knowing that just down the hall Nash Buckingham and Herb Parsons were arguing the fine points of pass shooting.

"Mr. Nash" had been feeling blue. The mallard flight was lighter than usual that autumn, his shooting eye was dimming (he was over 80 then, and it had taken him all of an hour to limit out that day) and he was mourning the old red-letter days at his beloved Beaver Dam. As a result of all this, the concluding lines of the small book on mallards was a mix of his nostalgic pessimism and my own youthful optimism.

> *It's painful to know that our waterfowl resource is threadbare and that the great abundances faded so quickly, so easily. Painful, too, is the knowledge that we are no longer young hunters in a young land. We have spent our youth and much of our natural wealth in a headlong rush of technology. We are children prematurely gray, still looking wistfully backward and reluctant to admit that our boyhood heroes – the Dood Gilberts and Fred Kimbles – have passed, and with them the immeasurable flights of wildfowl.*
>
> *But in place of youth and its openhanded waste, there are the first signs of maturity and a growing caution. A new wind is rising, fanning the embers of old camp fires, and we are slowly beginning to shape a national conservation conscience . . .*

That was written in 1961, just as we were sliding into a mallard depression. Nash had reason to feel low. But while none of us knew it at the time, there was to be reason for hope. Within a few years, a wildlifer named Dale Whitesell would leave the Ohio Division of Wildlife to assume leadership of Ducks Unlimited – and DU would be galvanized into the world's most dynamic citizen conservation effort.

It wouldn't be the first citizen effort to help restore the flights of North American wildfowl. One group, the old American Wild Fowlers, was organized in 1927. Nash Buckingham was hired as its field secretary the following year, and the Wild Fowlers racked up some solid achievements, including new federal game refuge legislation. By 1931 the American Wild Fowlers was absorbed by Joseph P. Knapp's rapidly growing More Game Birds in America Foundation, which, in turn, was expanded and reorganized as Ducks Unlimited in 1937.

From the first, Ducks Unlimited was an idea that worked. To be sure, there were a lot of great ideas taking shape in the mid-1930s. State game and fish agencies were being set up under bipartisan commissions, lifting them out of purely political control. Cooperative wildlife research units were being formed at some land grant colleges, and the units would train a new breed of wildlife biologist. The duck stamp act was passed. The National Wildlife Federation was born. The Pittman-Robertson Federal Aid in Wildlife Restoration Act became law. But DU stood alone as a volunteer citizen effort with one aim: to save the vital marshes that support North America's waterfowl.

Ducks Unlimited was born out of the drought and dust of the "Duckless Thirties," generating enthusiasm, money and wetlands for waterfowl. But it would be 28 years later, in 1965, that the idea would really catch fire. The year Whitesell came to DU, the group boasted less than 100 chapters, and had raised a total of $876,000 "for the ducks."

Today there are over 3,700 DU chapters, and in 1985 they generated $46.4 million.

Ducks Unlimited's effectiveness is simplicity itself. Its energy has been directed toward the saving and managing of wetlands that would otherwise have been bled in the name of progress. It is a direct route without the boggy detours and foggy vision that have undone so many other well-intentioned conservation efforts. It's a chance for any hunter to have a direct, personal piece of the action, knowing that of every dollar contributed to DU nearly 80 cents will be spent out there on the marshes.

Certain critics, of course, grumble that there's nothing un-selfish about any of this. They accuse the hunter of saving wetlands only to further his own selfish end of shooting ducks. Even if this were the whole truth, which it is not, it makes no difference to a nesting mallard. The only thing that matters to her is having a marsh on which to nest – a marsh which might not be there were its fate left to critics long on wind and short on commitment.

But more than the character of DU's programs or leader-ship, its success stems from the character of its membership – those tough, stubborn, opinionated, hard-nosed, mud-smeared, canvas-clad masochists called "duck hunters."

This is the solid base on which Ducks Unlimited is built. Of course, there should never be any doubt that all duck hunters are a little crazy. How else can you possibly explain them? But what fine madness it is! And what a bland, spirit-less world this would be without it, and without the marsh-lands and flights of wildfowl that it has given us.

John Madson
Godfrey, Illinois

PREFACE

Fifty years ago, Ducks Unlimited recognized the need to intervene in a positive way to restore waterfowl habitat ravaged by poor land-use policies and a prolonged drought. Since then DU's first project in Canada, Big Grass Marsh, has come to symbolize the organization's commitment to conserving North America's wetlands. For half a century, DU has remained steadfast to its singleness of purpose, adhering to the simple premise that properly restored and managed wetland habitat holds the key to abundant continental waterfowl.

Like nature, man too is ever-changing. As civilization clamors for more living space, the conservation of natural resources becomes even more crucial. But some things never change—like a duck's dependence on healthy breeding, staging and wintering habitat. Because the needs of the resource are fairly static and continental in scope, DU continues to pursue new and creative ways to provide waterfowl with their age-old habitat requirements. In many instances, what is good for waterfowl is also good for man. Wetlands prevent floods, purify air and water, recharge aquifers and relieve the impact of drought while quenching industry's and agriculture's thirst for fresh water.

Ignoring geographic and political boundaries, a duck seeks life-sustaining habitat wherever it can be found. Acutely aware of this, Ducks Unlimited's habitat efforts reach into every corner of the continent as it works in concert with conservation organizations from many nations. Cooperative agreements between these groups enable DU to restore wetland habitat essential to waterfowl throughout their annual life cycle—from where they nest to where they rest.

As a growing world places more demands on the land, nature's ability to sustain abundant waterfowl populations will depend in large part on man's ability to manage the remaining resources wisely. Cooperating with state, local and federal governments, DU is working its way across the vital prairie breeding grounds of Canada and the United States. Biologists estimate that upwards of six million more acres of these fertile prairie wetlands will be required to stabilize continental waterfowl populations. After half a century of hard work, DU has reserved about half this amount—acreage involving nearly 3,000 wetland projects and over 15,000 miles of nesting shoreline.

In order to accelerate habitat inventory efforts and evaluate potential new project areas on the breeding grounds, DU has harnessed the space telemetry of NASA's Landsat 5 satellite. From 450 miles above the earth, the orbiting satellite can pinpoint wetlands as small as a quarter-acre, enabling DU biologists to efficiently identify and evaluate potential habitat areas. In this way, DU can bring Landsat's sophisticated technology down to earth for the ducks. This application of scientific data will not only help secure a healthier habitat base for waterfowl, but for other wildlife as well.

Ducks Unlimited has indeed come a long way from the simple wooden dams it built to help restore Big Grass Marsh half a century ago. Utilizing the best of both worlds, nature's and man's, DU's biological and engineering staff continues to explore new methods of enhancing North America's wetlands.

Filled with all of its uncertainties and challenges, the future still belongs to those who dare to roll up their sleeves and join in the work at hand. To this end, Ducks Unlimited's singleness of purpose will progress into the next half-century, a tribute to those farsighted sportsmen who dared to roll up their sleeves back in 1937.

Dale E. Whitesell
Executive Vice President
Ducks Unlimited, Inc.

INTRODUCTION

The process of putting together any book is never simple, and *Return to Big Grass* was no exception to be sure. But something I think its readers will discover is that the writers, in carrying out their respective assignments, have succeeded in capturing an overall feel for Ducks Unlimited – a sense of the spirit which has made the outfit tick for 50 years. This spirit has to do with a deep-rooted concern on the part of DU volunteers for the preservation of North America's wetlands, and an enthusiastic consensus that these environments are worth carefully tending, even if doing so requires a great deal of energy and no small cost.

For this reason *Return to Big Grass* focuses more often than not on wetlands and man's interaction with them than it does on historic documentation of the growth of Ducks Unlimited itself. The book, then, is different from what you might have expected to find in a volume heralding the fiftieth anniversary of an organization. It is a celebration of DU, as well as an odyssey – a spiritual return to Big Grass Marsh, DU's first wetland project.

When DU Senior Writer Mike Beno traveled to the town of Gladstone, Manitoba, in June 1985, he wanted to find some physical remnants of the initial construction begun there in 1938. He knew that in addition to two dams, a small cabin had been erected on Big Grass Marsh. Along with the cabin was a lookout tower, and he figured that with luck and a little help from local people he might come upon some clues confirming the nearly 50-year-ago existence of both.

What Beno came up with was the keystone section of this book. Thanks to leads generated by Mike's friend – the late Jimmy Robinson of *Sports Afield* – Mike met a host of Canadian characters, each with his own ties to Big Grass Marsh. There was, for starters, George Scott. Jimmy remembered hearing that Scott had boarded the men who constructed the cabin on Big Grass in the winter of 1938. What Jimmy could not recall was Scott's whereabouts. Robinson remedied this by rallying the Royal Canadian Mounted Police, and they located Scott and others who proved helpful to Mike.

This section of *Return to Big Grass* is special, for it is here that readers will become familiar with the historical texture of DU. In addition to history, however, they will be treated to something more, for woven into the pages of this introductory chapter are rich, colorful shadings of the personalities who were to shape the future of Ducks Unlimited.

–Richard Wentz
Editor, Return to Big Grass

RETURN TO BIG GRASS

By Mike Beno

It felt like we were looking for forts, but Ted Code couldn't have known that.

I had not had the feeling in nearly 20 years, so it took awhile to puzzle it through as Code and I walked in silence, eyes scanning the ground, looking down into the tall June grasses of the Manitoba prairie. With occasional foot sweeps the Canadian duck hunter and I searched for a sign, for something out of place, for anything at all, as Mindy, his playful black Lab, snapped happily at flies.

"I think this is where the cabin was . . . the tower too, eh," Code said, as we stepped across telltale overgrown ruts and zeroed-in on the only wooded clump in sight, a patch of trees jutting into the flat miles, the open miles, the running-forever miles of waving emerald marsh hay.

But the feeling . . .

It was a back-home feeling. I mean a *way* back-home feeling. A nostalgic, treasure-hunt, little brother kind of feeling. Though he was only five years old – five full years younger than I – my little brother was a nomad. Particularly ramblative for his stumpy legs, he'd often pioneer blocks beyond the bounds that would earn parental poundings.

All older brothers know that a younger brother is an invention with limited purpose: a nickname target, a receptacle for derision, the butt of rotten jokes. All in all he is to be as avoided as a bucket of rats – except when he *has* something. Like a fort.

Little brothers never learn. Time after time, well-oiled with material promise, he would lead me to his secret places. And time after time I claimed them as my own, though his creative names generally stuck. A grove of trees: The Green Apple Fort; a non-wheeled, 1950ish pickup abandoned to rot: The Junker Fort; plywood scraps crammed creatively into a culvert; The Hole Fort. But you quickly learn that *having* the fort is never near as fun as when you first found it.

Ranging far ahead, Mindy at his side, Code swatted mosquitoes and continued looking. Was this the yard? If so, a lot of people had been around here for a lot of years. They would have left something behind.

Keep looking.

A clear patch in the grass was enough to quicken my pulse. *Wood!*

Weathered with grayness, nailed together, the small platform sat sunken in the prairie sod. A footing? A tower pad? A well cover? A trap door?

I wished for a spade, but a stick would work. That's it . . . get in under the edge . . . pry . . . yes, there it is. Now pulllll . . .

Giving with a stubborn rip, the wood-rot specimen split, revealing both the ground and the junior archaeologist's simplicity.

Keep looking.

"Mike!" Code yelled, now kneeling in the grass, "Concrete! I got concrete!"

Cracked and crumbling, the white slab sitting in the middle of the wooded patch was grown through with grasses and bushes and little elm trees. An aged trailer tongue lay rusting amid scattered orts. Like kids hunting eggs on Easter morning, the scramble was on.

"An old trap pad," said Code, handing over a rusted disc. "Wonder how that got here?"

More walking brought more concrete, a straight piece, and another, and a broken foundation corner. "Don't step there," Code warned, pointing down at the grassed-over shaft sunk deep into the ground. "Looks like the corner of the building, or a well . . . or . . . something. But I think this is it. I think we found it."

1

RETURN TO BIG GRASS

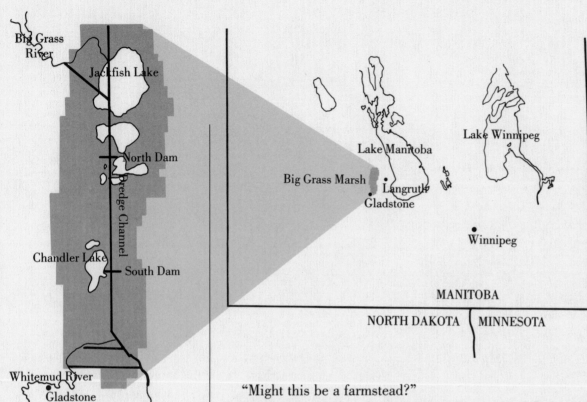

"Might this be a farmstead?"

"A farmstead? No, this has to be it," an excited Code said, hustling Mindy back toward his truck. "Mind you, settlers didn't have concrete. I'll bet that's where the cabin sat. Anyway, I *think* this is it. Tomorrow we'll drive out to Langruth and find somebody who knows for sure. My friend Bob Gass will help us, he's a constable with the RCMP."

Swatting Manitoba mosquitoes, we climbed back into the truck grinning with the certainty that we had found the old, storied cabin site of Ducks Unlimited's first project, begun 50 years ago on Big Grass Marsh. We had found Duck Factory Number One.

Or had we?

For 50 years Ducks Unlimited, Inc. has held firmly to its singleness of purpose – a belief that control of water on the wetlands which produce and sustain North America's wild ducks and geese is essential for their propagation. It is on this tenet of active wildlife management that DU has flourished.

Since it was incorporated on January 29, 1937, DU has grown to become a global force in wildlife conservation. Over a half-million members, spread the world over, count themselves part of the success story. In its first year, DU's 6,270 members from 27 states raised $90,000 – far short of the $126,500 estimated need for 1938's conservation expenditures. Today, that need could be fulfilled in a single evening's worth of a volunteer fund-raising event. In 1985, 3,624 volunteer DU committees helped raise $46.4 million for waterfowl conservation.

From the beginning DU's official purpose has been *to raise money for developing, preserving, restoring and maintaining the waterfowl habitat on the North American continent*. While money makes many worlds go around, it is only part of the story. The second half of DU's stated purpose – the developing, preserving, restoring and maintaining – is the most critical part of the organization's work. Today DU is the only organization of its kind. Nonprofit, nongovernmental, it undertakes a unique kind of wetland habitat work – a careful manipulation of water levels which provides optimum living conditions for over 300 wildlife species in addition to ducks and geese.

The genesis of this conservation ethic can be traced to 1912. Unlike today, when all wildlife is seen to have worth, game animals were the only conservation beneficiaries around the turn of the century. Game was valued, vermin was not; a simplistic view, but a good start. The Game Conservation Society was founded that year in New York by Dwight W. Huntington, an attorney. Huntington also edited *Amateur Sportsman*, a popular sporting magazine of the day whose motto was "More game and fewer game laws."

Irked by the idea that a licensed hunter could take hundreds of quail, yet could not legally raise them to put anything back, Huntington's ideas on conservation were tied to the old European practice of gamekeeping. To that end, The Game Conservation Society founded a gamekeeper's school. Established at Clinton, New Jersey, in 1928, The Conservation Institute was financed by donations from the sporting arms industry. Under the guidance of James Craven, "a practical English gamekeeper of long experience," the school's 25 students raised 4,080 pheasants, 195 ducks, 380 quail and 100 other birds during that first year.

The gamekeeper's school had no peer, for there were not even any textbooks on game breeding or game management at the time. The school received some faculty assistance from Rutgers University, but struggled financially. In the fall of 1930, however, a special visitor arrived.

Joseph Palmer Knapp of New York was a big-business printing magnate, philanthropist and a Currituck Sound duck shooter of note. Today, Knapp is regarded as the father of Ducks Unlimited. Aggressive in the extreme, Knapp began his business career as a salesman for his father's lithographic firm in 1881. Within 10 years he had purchased his father's interest, and a year later, absorbed a dozen competitors. He eventually printed the rotogravure sections of half the newspapers in the United States. In 1906, he purchased Crowell publishing company, and in 1919 he acquired control of *Collier's* weekly and the book publisher P. F. Collier and Son. Life insurance and securities came later.

A benefactor of education and conservation, Knapp made anonymous donations for both causes. The old duck shot was so taken with the ideas of scientific game management as practiced at the gamekeeper's school that he started the More Game Birds in America Foundation. The foundation assumed full management of the foundering school, but did not shoulder its financial responsibilities. Knapp himself, however,

Joseph Palmer Knapp—printer, publisher and progenitor of Ducks Unlimited. Political cartoonist Jay N. "Ding" Darling called Knapp "The Sage of Currituck, who was one of the best wing shots and has spent more of his personal fortune on ducks than any man in the United States."

stepped into the breech with huge donations to keep the school afloat. It eventually closed its doors in 1935.

Huntington's son, John C., and Arthur W. Bartley were made executives of More Game Birds, and under the foundation's bylaws, a minimum of 25 directors were appointed. Political cartoonist J. N. "Ding" Darling and financier J. Pierpont Morgan were two of them.

As Knapp pushed, so pushed the foundation. An extension of the aggressive publisher, More Game Birds pumped prose. During its eight years of existence, it produced 12 booklets on game birds and game bird breeding.

More Game Birds was a strong advocate of the user-pay principle of wildlife management, and in 1932, proposed a cent-a-shell tax on shotgun ammunition. The idea never went anywhere, but it helped boost the concept of tying costs of wetland habitat maintenance to the user. This culminated in the enactment of the federal duck stamp in 1934.

Another concept bannered by More Game Birds was extensive management of waterfowl breeding grounds. Specific suggestions to this end included: "maintenance of water levels as directed by engineers; provision of food and cover

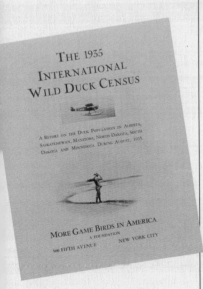

THE 1935 INTERNATIONAL WILD DUCK CENSUS

A REPORT ON THE DUCK POPULATION IN ALBERTA, SASKATCHEWAN, MANITOBA, NORTH DAKOTA, SOUTH DAKOTA AND MINNESOTA DURING AUGUST, 1935.

MORE GAME BIRDS IN AMERICA
A FOUNDATION
500 FIFTH AVENUE   NEW YORK CITY

North America's first large-scale duck census covered 995,631 square miles in prairie Canada and the United States.

Part of the census crew (from left): C.S. Bedell, director of upland game bird activities, More Game Birds in America Foundation; Cec McNeal, pilot; A.C. Camerle, director of waterfowl activities, More Game Birds; Carl Yule, pilot; John C. Huntington and Arthur Bartley, executives of More Game Birds.

dian breeding grounds. The area covered 762,497 square miles in Canada and 233,134 in the United States. The organization's ambitious intentions were announced in mid-July, and by August, the survey was underway.

Game officials from the prairie provinces, the Dakotas and Minnesota promised full cooperation after receiving telegraphed inquiries. Groundwork involved state, county and local conservation groups. Landowners were enlisted as well. Some 1,500 individuals, mostly farmers, returned census questionnaires.

But the most remembered aspect of the survey was the aerial portion. Nearly 14,000 air miles were logged in three weeks, from the agricultural lands surrounding Big Grass Marsh, as far north as Great Slave Lake, in the MacKenzie District of the Northwest Territories.

Surveyors included Bartley who covered Alberta, John Huntington who covered Manitoba, and A. C. Camerle – director of waterfowl activities for the foundation – who covered Saskatchewan. Small, hand-held cameras were used to make hundreds of pictures of wooded lakes, broad marshes, small outposts and ducks.

The survey's most important findings were these. First, the 1935 duck crop stood at about 42,700,000 birds – a number thought to be the largest in six years. Water had returned to some spots on the prairies. The survey's second finding was the reinforced belief that the prairie breeding grounds were the keystone in the propagation of North America's waterfowl. The doctor had diagnosed the problem. After the survey, More Game Birds reported:

There is now no escaping the logical conclusion that unless prompt action is taken to preserve Canadian breeding grounds the future of wildfowling in the United States hangs in a precarious balance ... the more the results of the

by caring for existing growth, introducing new varieties, preventing fires, eliminating grazing; preventing trespassing; controlling natural enemies where necessary; using sanitation to check disease."

Duck shooters one and all, the early directors of More Game Birds were dismayed by the decline in ducks they had witnessed during the drought of the "Dirty Thirties." They were determined to do something about it. But before work could be done on the patient, the doctor had to diagnose the problem.

Called the granddad of waterfowl surveys, the 1935 International Wild Duck Census was a massive undertaking by More Game Birds. It was the first aerial survey of the Cana-

Three amphibious, bush-piloted craft carried the surveyors.

International Wild Duck Census are studied, the more it becomes apparent that efforts from now on must center on waterfowl restoration in Canada. Recognizing the gravity of the situation, the foundation during the past fiscal year began work on development of a plan for preservation and restoration of Canadian breeding grounds. Ducks Unlimited will be the name of the new Canadian foundation. A tentative draft of the plan of operation has been presented to the premiers of Alberta, Saskatchewan and Manitoba, fish and game officials, and leading businessmen and sportsmen of the provinces. Most complimentary letters of endorsement and approval have been received from all concerned along with promises of complete cooperation.

More Game Birds assigned all its assets to the new organization. On April 1, 1938, Bartley met with a newly appointed eight-man board at the Fort Garry Hotel in Winnipeg. Bartley had been named the first executive director of Ducks Unlimited, Inc. The business of the meeting was the organization of DU's Canadian arm, which would supply the biological and engineering muscle, but Bartley made it abundantly clear that he needed a project, and needed one bad.

DU had been in existence over one year. Fund-raising had begun, and if the program was to grow, it was imperative to show hard evidence to prospective contributors in the United States. If approximately 100,000 wetland acres could be restored on the prairie breeding grounds of Canada, Bartley said, with before-and-after pictures taken to show what had been accomplished, the job of selling the program in the Sunny South would be much easier.

Bartley's Canadian friends put themselves to it. The first staff meeting of Ducks Unlimited Canada was held on Wednesday, April 20, 1938 in Winnipeg. The business of the meeting was to establish the hatchling organization's 1938 program. Attending were Tommy Main, general manager; Don Stephens, Manitoba supervisor; Bert Cartwright, chief naturalist; and Dorothy Cartwright, stenographer.

Three large potential waterfowl habitat restoration projects were planned, one for each of the three prairie provinces: Big Grass Marsh, Manitoba; Waterhen Marsh, Saskatchewan; and Many Island Lake, Alberta. The next day, April 21, Cartwright, Main and Stephens inspected Big Grass. Within 10 days of the establishment of DU Canada's office, a temporary dam was built on the marsh.

As sparse as the trees in the sprawling hay-and-grain territory off the southwest shore of Lake Manitoba, only a few tiny towns have acquired ringside seats edging Big Grass Marsh. Set off Manitoba Highway 16, southwest of the marsh, Gladstone rests in a green sea of fields dotted with picturesque grain elevators, crisscrossed by train tracks. *Clack-clack!* say the mile-long Canadian National freights, keeping constant tempo like monstrous metronomes. *Clack-clack!* say the mile-long Canadian Pacific freights, wailing long and lonely into the dark prairie nights, grain-gorged cannister cars bound for Winnipeg, then Thunder Bay.

Depending on with whom you speak, and age has everything to do with this, you'll hear different definitions of The Marsh. Talk with Gladstone resident Ted Code or RCMP constable Bob Gass, and they will tell you the marsh is a 27,000-acre tract that DU calls its first project, and that the Manitoba government calls a "Class A" bird sanctuary. But climb into Gass' Bronco and join the Gladstoners on a tour of the marsh and you will hear a grander, more colorful definition of Big Grass. First stop is the farmyard of 77-year-old Ed Hoehn.

A turn-of-the-century wave of settlers followed the railroad

RETURN TO BIG GRASS

Bulrush, cattail, and sedge on Jackfish Lake, the most open part of Big Grass Marsh. The marsh was named for its 10-foot stands of vegetation.

west in 1896, and when Hoehn's parents first settled the farm he works today, they saw a massive marsh engulfing 100,000 acres, draining an area in excess of 920 square miles. Named by Indians for the 10-foot-high rushes it supported, Big Grass supported many settlers as well. The new residents found abundance in the marsh, its marginal lands suited to cropping, its rangeland filled with hay, its waters a life-giving gift — a gift later foolishly shunned.

Herding their oxen onto train cars in Winnipeg, the exodus of young homesteaders traveled 100 miles. Landing in Gladstone, they gathered their possessions and drove the oxen north to the marsh.

Big Grass Marsh, at its most basic, is a basin — a remnant of the ancient bed of Lake Agassiz. Varying in size and changing with the ages, the great glacial lake covered 180,000

square miles at different times, an area larger than California. Most of Manitoba was covered at one time or another, as well as parts of Saskatchewan, Ontario, Minnesota and the Dakotas. Formed during the Pleistocene era, some 10,000 years ago, Lake Agassiz has left its mark on the land. The shores are still visible in sand and gravel deposits — beach ridges that can be traced for hundreds of miles. The 40-mile-wide Big Grass basin lies between the Riding Mountains on the west and the beachhead of Lake Manitoba on the east. The Big Grass basin serves as a watershed for the hazy, gray mountains that rise some 30 miles distant, flushing waters east toward Lake Manitoba. The waters feed Big Grass Marsh which, in turn, helps slow them.

"When my father came here in 1905," says Gilman Watson, another west-side farmer with historical perspective, "this was a homesteader's paradise. There was fish and there was wood and there was game. You could go out and get all the geese you wanted." Watson ambles across his yard as Lucky, the big white saddle horse, cautiously watches. "The hotel in town would buy geese from hunters — but my father used what he got," says Watson. "He'd bury the meat in oats or hang it in the well to keep."

Unable to coax Lucky closer, Watson stops and looks across the open vista spread before him. "I don't ride him anymore — he's too damn much horse for me. But I used to take saddle horses and teams all over the marsh," he says. It was always difficult to judge direction when crossing the broad marsh on a run for wood. Nighttime, of course, was especially bad, so when teams went out, it was customary to hang a lantern from the Willow Bush. Still growing today, it continues to be the only brush clump visible for miles.

"It's one hell of a scary feeling to be lost on that marsh. I got lost one night in 1933," says Watson. Hitching a pair of

6

colts to his wagon, young Watson left home in the afternoon, anxious to cut his load of wood. So anxious, in fact, he left without a coat. The long hours of Manitoba sunlight didn't quite stretch until 10 p.m. in the fall, and that was the time of evening he started back home with his load. It was at around 10:05 that the snowstorm struck. "It was freezing and I was driving blind," he says. "I couldn't see the road. All I could do was turn the colts loose and let 'em walk. There were no landmarks for them to see, nothing to follow, and they were getting played out." Their reins dragging free, following instinct alone, the colts bucked wind and snow for 10 freezing miles. Instinct alone was enough to bring the green colts and their exhausted driver back to the farmyard sometime near dawn.

Though dangerous if not respected, the marsh is seen by many as the greatest natural resource a district could want, and the key is water. "Times were good when I was a lit-

tle shaver," Watson says. "You could live like a king off the land. My father had four or five wells on his hog farm. All you had to do was go down 10 feet for all the water you could ever use."

Once they'd put a few years of agricultural progress behind them, the hard-working marshland settlers had it easier than when they arrived. Cereal grains needed room for cultivation. Cattle and sheep needed room for hay. Money was waiting to be made.

Though the scheme was not begun until 1910, the Manitoba government first contracted to drain Big Grass Marsh in 1880. The Manitoba North Western Drainage Company, with W. E. Sanford as chief, undertook the job. American land speculators were involved, rolling up their sleeves at a dinner table set by a law which provided that he who drained the land received half of it. Thus the name W. E. Sanford is emblazoned on the plat maps across many homesteads. Rural

Called "Big Lake" in 1906, Big Grass Marsh provided recreation for settlers. This summer regatta was held near the present Chandler Lake, on the marsh's south end.

RETURN TO BIG GRASS

Farmer Gilman Watson and Lucky.

municipalities still sent tax bills to long-lost American owners until the mid-1970s.

The American real estate syndicate's report estimated that 150,000 to 200,000 acres of agricultural land would be available if the marsh were lowered six feet. Work began in August 1910, the provincial government investing upwards of $1 million. The people of the district eagerly drove their draft horses out to watch the action as two mighty floating dredges tore at the basin, ripping a nine-foot-deep channel through the heart of the marsh. Big booms swinging, the coal-fired behemoths belched black smoke and hauled up earth. The plan was this: to channel the water quickly to the south and out of Big Grass Marsh to eliminate the slowing action of the

watershed. The marsh was made a chute instead of a sponge, speeding heavy spring waters to Lake Manitoba.

There was no opposition to the project for it promised riches and provided employment. Settlers Bill Armstrong and Bill Hill were responsible for stockpiling coal along the routes used by the snorting diggers.

Mr. Sanford, too, did a hell of job. By the end of 1912, 253 miles of ditches were gorged out, directly affecting 394,000 acres. By 1913, the northerly Grassy River, which had fed the marsh, was connected by ditches to the southerly Whitemud River, which drained the area. Three smaller "walking" dredges had carved lateral channels east and west. Sluicing down these tubes went the waters gifted to the settlers; rushing away went the life of the wetland. Big Grass Marsh had died . . . and nobody came to the funeral. The sentiment of the day, as mirrored in *The Gladstone Age Press*, October 30, 1913:

> *Already the effects of the work done so far are most noticeable, and residents of the district say that it is only a matter of a short time when Big Grassy Marsh, as such, will have entirely disappeared. With this gone and the lateral drains bringing the adjacent territory in shape for settlement, the whole of the district will soon be in the position of having no waste land. It has long been recognized that this drained land is among the most valuable in the province, for it possesses a store of crop-producing elements which appear inexhaustible. While the sportsmen of the province have lost a grand duck shooting ground at Big Grassy Marsh the province has gained thousands of acres of land which will produce returns on a valuation of millions of dollars.*

"When they drained that bloody marsh it was the worst mistake ever made," crows Watson with an agitated sneer.

Dredging the Whitemud River, 1906. Fired with coal, this floating dredge straightened the river into which Big Grass Marsh drained, speeding its waters to Lake Manitoba. A second dredge ripped a 9-foot-deep ditch down the center of the marsh to channel water out.

"They buggered everything up and we're still payin' for it." Watson first noticed something was wrong when, as a little shaver, he went to the well in the front yard of his father's farm and walked away thirsty. Shrugging their collective shoulders, the family simply went to the hog pasture a few yards away where there were four more wells. Those held out for around a week. Then, Watson grunts, "they all went dry, every damn one of 'em." With the source of groundwater recharge gone, the water table had reacted with vengeance. "Years ago you never heard of short water," Watson says. "Well, we have it yet in some places."

Hand-dug wells, 50 feet deep and 4 feet square, failed like the 10-footers did. In the 1920s, farmers began hauling their water. And the drier it got, the farther they hauled.

"Once this got dry, it made a difference," says Watson's neighbor Ed Hoehn. "People began to think twice about the marsh then. There were no wells. There wasn't a drop in the creek or marsh. It's no damn fun when you come back from work with a team of horses and there's no water."

The big marsh grasses so relied upon by cattle ranchers and sheep herders were long gone, and grain crops were moribund. Hoehn recalls: "Some of the stock was nothing but a skeleton, and a neighbor of mine had three of his horses hanging in slings at one time because they couldn't stand."

Land was going for $1.50 per acre during the drought of the Dirty Thirties. Even at that price it was not affordable, as broke farmers walked away from their tax-burdened acreage. Until he could afford land, Watson says, he simply squatted on abandoned property. After the marsh was drained, the populace awoke to find that survey lines had been completed, and the bulk of the land was owned by American speculators. But the drought did not care. It steamrollered monied investors as surely as it did the lowliest Canadian dirt farmer, and when the Americans gave up and went home, their mighty $30,000 dredges lay rotting where they stopped work.

Instead of becoming the Fertile Crescent of Canada, the Big Grass basin was a ruin. No crops would grow in the soils—not even marsh hay. Gone were the waving grasses that inspired the Indians, the waving grasses that the ox-drawn settlers saw. Gone were the ducks, gone were the geese, gone were the deer that Watson's father hunted.

"The vegetation used to be so high, you couldn't see where you were going with your horse and buggy." Watson says. "But when they drained it, all of that died. It was just peat out there . . . peat three or four feet deep." Far from the soils with "inexhaustible" elements that had been promised, the peat

9

was little more than an inexhaustible fuel source. As the ground dried, it caught fire. And acre after acre, year after year, it burned across the miles.

"The peat fires burned underneath the surface," Watson explains. "But the smoke was hard to see sometimes, and there might be just a little shell on the top. Quite often, your teams would break through that crust and it'd singe 'em to the knees. Our saddle horses, when we drove cattle, they'd fall through too. The fires burned day and night, summer and winter." In the winter, Watson says, it was easier to spot the treacherous places. Whether smoke curled upward or not, you learned to avoid the yellow patches in the snow.

All vegetation gone, the burned-out basin blew silt. It was a gray silt that formed gray clouds and piled up in big, gray ridges. Some of the ridges are still visible. Ashes and dust and silt and stones lay in the withered beds of Jackfish Lake and Chandler Lake, the deepest parts of the basin—the heart of Big Grass Marsh.

Hoehn still recalls the erosion and curses what caused it. "I had 11 sections, and I always left a quarter of each for wildlife. Those big farmers, the ones with the big tillers, they told me I was crazy. 'Look at all the money you could make on those bushes!' Well, now I've got the burden—all the fox and sharptail and deer live in those bushes and every Tom, Dick and Harry wants in to hunt 'em. Even the farmers that plowed all the bush off their land."

In 1932, Hoehn says, he took a dead-center walk on a direct line right across the marsh—a west sider heading east to see some of the Icelanders at Langruth. It was the shortest trip to the east side he ever made. "It was about 10 or 15 miles across the marsh. I never got my feet wet." Over that hot, sun-beaten distance Hoehn saw this: silt, weeds, dust, stones, a Russian thistle and one lost seagull. "And just a few years before," Hoehn says, "the mallards came out of there like smoke."

Not surprisingly, Hoehn found the east side of the marsh faring no better than the west. Water and wildlife were gone, the drought was as strong as ever, the depression was felt by all. At a cent per pound, it was not unusual for a rancher to ship cattle to Winnipeg and receive only a bill for freight.

"Years ago you never heard of short water," says Gilman Watson. "Well, we have it yet in some places."

John Arnason's dam—hammered-in poles stuffed with hay.

"Was it tough? It was tough all right. There was no money, if that's what you mean," says George Scott, an east-side rancher from Langruth. "You didn't make any money, you just found enough to live on."

Continuing our tour of the marsh, Code, Gass and I have landed in tiny Langruth. The search for old-timers who know something of the marsh's history has led to Scott, 74, and Pete Skoropata, 70, a couple of cattle-and-sheep men who ranched the rough years. Sitting amid the noontime clatter in the cafe at the Langruth Hotel, full of feverishly lunching construction workers, the ranchers remember when the marsh was not a marsh.

"Where was that cabin?" an inquisitive Code asks the ranchers, too anxious to sit through hard-time stories.

"We'll take you there later," Scott says.

Scott quit grain farming in the early thirties, thinking cattle and sheep more profitable. "If you broke your car down you'd go maybe a year before you'd get it going again. I remember the last year we farmed, we had all kinds of granaries full of barley. You'd haul a load of grain to Portage la Prairie with a team of horses and get $5.50 for the whole wagonload. *Seven cents a bushel*. The bearings on my car went bad, and one bearing cost me $8.00. That's how tough it was. I hauled about 10 loads of grain in with the horses before I got the old Model A going again."

When Scott moved marshside in 1937, it was an isolated area, five or six families living in the vicinity. Big Grass Marsh was a burning waste. The basin was so dry, Scott recalls, that he took his Model A across one of the drainage ditches and on tour through the marsh. "We had no water. We had trouble getting water for our cattle... we tried sloughs... anything. Wells you couldn't depend on. We hauled our drinking water from town."

Looking for any means to moisture, ranchers excavated dugouts to hold rainwater. These pits, however, were only as dependable as rain. Scott's neighbor, John Arnason, came up with another idea. With poles and hay and straw and earth he dammed one of the abandoned dredge canals. Little more than a makeshift beaver pile, the dam held about a foot of water – when any was available. The dam likely had a dual purpose: stock water and the return of muskrats. Arnason was a hunter and trapper.

A hunter, trapper and maybe a bit of a prairie playboy, John Arnason got around. The bachelor sheep and cattle rancher trod the six-mile bridle path from the marsh into Langruth on a much more regular basis than Scott or Skoropata.

"We were working people, and so was John, but he would

Big Grass Marsh, 1938.

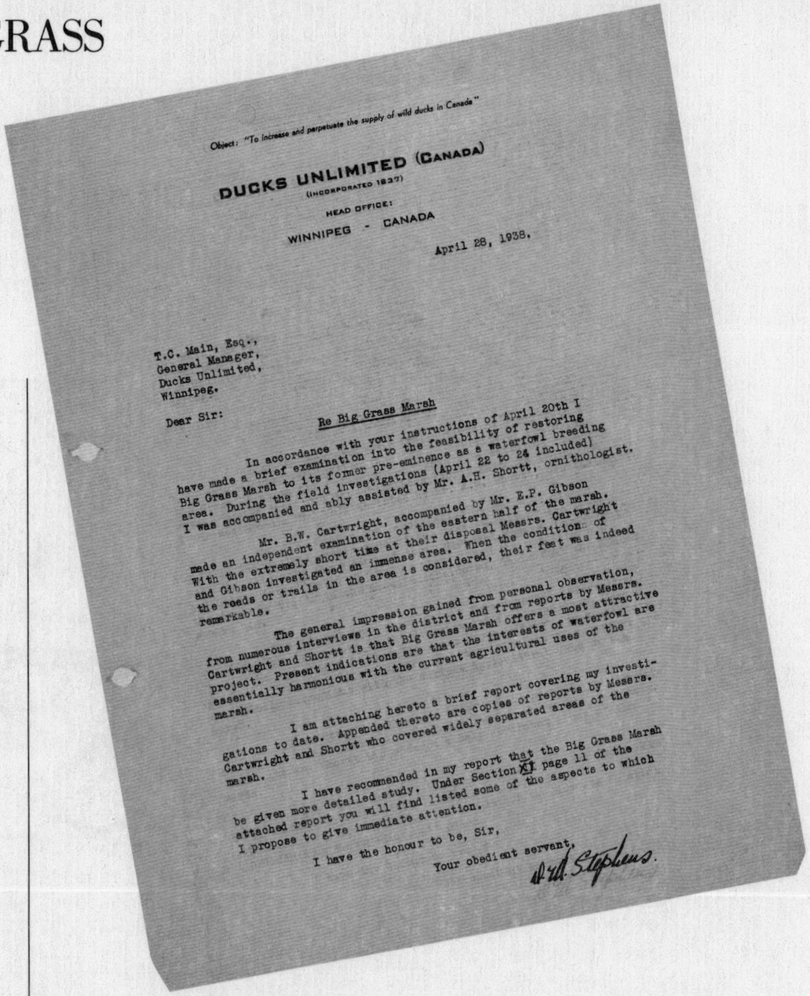

Object: "To increase and perpetuate the supply of wild ducks in Canada"

DUCKS UNLIMITED (CANADA)
(INCORPORATED 1937)
HEAD OFFICE:
WINNIPEG - CANADA

April 28, 1938.

T.C. Main, Esq.,
General Manager,
Ducks Unlimited,
Winnipeg.

Dear Sir:

Re Big Grass Marsh

In accordance with your instructions of April 20th I have made a brief examination into the feasibility of restoring Big Grass Marsh to its former pre-eminence as a waterfowl breeding area. During the field investigations (April 22 to 24 included) I was accompanied and ably assisted by Mr. A.H. Shortt, ornithologist.

Mr. B.W. Cartwright, accompanied by Mr. E.P. Gibson made an independent examination of the eastern half of the marsh. With the extremely short time at their disposal Messrs. Cartwright and Gibson investigated an immense area. When the conditions of the roads or trails in the area is considered, their feat was indeed remarkable.

The general impression gained from personal observation, from numerous interviews in the district and from reports by Messrs. Cartwright and Shortt is that Big Grass Marsh offers a most attractive project. Present indications are that the interests of waterfowl are essentially harmonious with the current agricultural uses of the marsh.

I am attaching hereto a brief report covering my investigations to date. Appended thereto are copies of reports by Messrs. Cartwright and Shortt who covered widely separated areas of the marsh.

I have recommended in my report that the Big Grass Marsh be given more detailed study. Under Section XI page 11 of the attached report you will find listed some of the aspects to which I propose to give immediate attention.

I have the honour to be, Sir,

Your obedient servant,

D.A. Stephens.

Ducks Unlimited Manitoba supervisor Don Stephens' letter to general manager Tommy Main. Four days later, on May 2, Stephens hired Bill Campbell to survey the marsh.

take time off for a drink," says Skoropata. "He was one of those chaps that didn't care too much about what he had. He'd take all summer off going to picnics or horse races—stuff like that. Lotta times, he'd run into people right here in the hotel. Ended up staying here a lot."

"John spent a lot of time at our place," says Scott, "and he could talk. He'd tell me all about the new guys that were coming out to the marsh."

Even before he heard the local gossip, Scott knew something was up. His Icelandic square-logged home, corral and outbuildings sat along one of the main thoroughfares, the Sandy Bay Trail. Still partly visible from his front yard, it stretched from the Sandy Bay Indian Reservation in the north, down to Gladstone. There were no roads.

During the most hectic, traffic-jammed days of summer, he'd see maybe 15 wagonloads of Indians pass by, en route to the annual Gladstone summer picnic. But on a regular day, he might count on seeing, well, no one. Cars motoring through the marsh grass, heading up the trail to Arnason's, were the first sign of activity.

Though Arnason told Scott, and all who would sit still to listen, about his new next-door neighbors from Winnipeg, Scott had no real contact with any DU personnel until December 1938. Little did he or Skoropata know, but they would later work with their new neighbors.

"I don't know when they built any dams," Scott says, "but I know when the cabin was built. I know it for a fact because the two chaps who built the cabin boarded at our place, in the old log house."

Yes, *technically*, it could be said they stayed in Scott's house. But actually the two slept in the only space available—a five-foot by five-foot woodshed/entryway that is tacked onto the side of the house that stands vacant today. But it was not too bad a bargain figuring the Winnipeg carpenters boarded for free, the alternative being winter nights on the prairie.

"They come out the first of December and started working their heads off," Scott says. "They were working overtime, they were working every night after supper by lamplight. They wanted to be out by Christmas and were scared they might get caught in the snow. They left the night before Christmas, and I'll tell you, they just barely got out. It was a beauty of a blizzard they left in."

Though Scott didn't know it, buckets of sweat had been shed long before the cabin went up at the end of 1938. In fact, three dams had been built on Big Grass Marsh, one of them within three miles of his ranch.

Bill Campbell, a powerfully built surveyor and engineer from Winnipeg, was the dynamo behind the dams. Campbell's assignment: stanch the flow of the lifeblood of Big

Grass Marsh. Hired by DU Manitoba Supervisor Don Stephens on May 2, 1938, he made the required surveys by May 4. The first dam, on the marsh's south end, was completed on May 10. Campbell had hired a crew of four who drove a line of timbers across the dredged ditch. Rocks were piled on either side of the timbers. It was a very temporary structure, but it held through the summer quite well. Ravaged Chandler Lake was a lake again.

With some relief in sight, the populace was pleased. A big change in attitude had occurred since 1913. *The Gladstone Age Press*, Thursday, May 12, 1938:

DUCKS UNLIMITED

What a wonderful name for a group of sportsmen whose object it is to perpetuate our splendid game birds in their natural breeding places. And the good news is that they are getting busy. For several weeks now their Mr. Stevens [sic] and a govt. surveyor, Mr. Wm. Campbell have been going over the Big Grass Marsh area, and now we are assured it will be one of the first projects to be developed for the breeding of ducks.

Farmers are assured no farmlands will be damaged and that adjacent haylands will be greatly improved by holding the water on the old lake bed, under a control gate dam. This should also mean work for many local men, and several permanent jobs as game and fire guardians.

The temporary dam in place, Campbell turned his attentions north, where Arnason had had a very worthy idea a few years before. Problem was, the well-intentioned shepherd was no engineer. His sievelike dam held only a foot of water in Jackfish Lake. In late fall, after the ground had dried sufficiently firm, yet before the frost made it too firm, Campbell and crew went to work. The engineer had completed more comprehensive contour surveys, and he chose a spot about

one mile south of the Arnason dam. Working out of a tent camp, Macaw and Macdonald, a Winnipeg contractor, started driving piles. Campbell lived with and oversaw the 10-man crew. Using horses to drag the 500-pound hammer up to the top of its travel, the crew constructed a new stoplog dam in the drainage ditch once plugged by Arnason's pile — the ditch that sucked the life from Big Grass Marsh. A similar dam was built to replace the temporary structure on Chandler Lake. Campbell made a daily hike of six miles, one way, to check the construction on the south dam. Both dams were completed by December 5. It took four full years, until 1942, for the marsh project to reach "full supply level," engineer's jargon that, roughly translated, meant Duck Factory Number One was in full operation.

In the meantime, DU Canada's first year in the duck factory business was booming. Charged on April 1 to build 100,000 acres of marshland, Tommy Main got at it. After Big Grass came Waterhen Marsh near Kinistino, Saskatchewan; then Many Island Lake in Medicine Hat, Alberta. Much as Big Grass Marsh, Waterhen called for correction of man's interference through misguided drainage. The 8,360-acre Many Island Lake project required more complex work to tame and trap floodwaters. Main himself took responsibility for this far-flung project. Later in the year the Stalwart Marsh, Ministik Lake and the Mormon Church Ranch were added as projects.

By year end, Main had not only met Bartley's acreage goal,

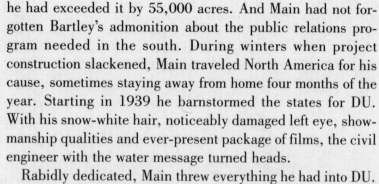

Tommy Main (in bow) tours Big Grass Marsh in the early 1940s. A former civil engineer in charge of water service and supplies for Canadian National Railways, Main came to his job with long experience in western Canadian water conservation.

he had exceeded it by 55,000 acres. And Main had not forgotten Bartley's admonition about the public relations program needed in the south. During winters when project construction slackened, Main traveled North America for his cause, sometimes staying away from home four months of the year. Starting in 1939 he barnstormed the states for DU. With his snow-white hair, noticeably damaged left eye, showmanship qualities and ever-present package of films, the civil engineer with the water message turned heads.

Rabidly dedicated, Main threw everything he had into DU. According to one story that was substantiated by his daughter, Main personally borrowed $25,000 to help the company through hard times during the war years.

In 1939, the first year of management on Big Grass, DU was making plans to extend its project horizon beyond the prairies, into the area that Tommy Main called "No Man's Land." Main proposed, and went ahead with, project work in a region north of the Precambrian Shield. Four projects were planned in the region from The Pas in northern Manitoba, to the Peace-Athabasca Delta in Northern Alberta.

While Main forged into the north, others held the program together in the south where Bert Cartwright played a major role. Bertram W. Cartwright was hired as DU Canada chief naturalist on May 1, 1938. Born in England, he emigrated to Winnipeg as a young man, where he became one of the founders of the Manitoba Natural History Society and the Manitoba Museum. A well-known authority on birds, he wrote a column called "Wild Wings" in the *Winnipeg Tribune*.

As Cartwright's first project, Big Grass Marsh was also his pet project. Initial management was intensive and a full-time manager was installed at the cabin in 1939. Cartwright made it his business to visit Langruth often, and every Langruth

old-timer seems to have a favorite Bert Story. The clean-cut man with the wire-rimmed glasses cut a decidedly urban figure, but all the locals accepted the gentleman English biologist, and today remember him with warmth.

"Bert had a bad stomach, and he'd often stop by our place for some milk," Scott remembers. "Bert always stayed at the cabin when he came out. I didn't see him every time, but sometimes, the way the roads were, I couldn't help but see him." Many were the occasions when Scott hitched up his "gray team" – four big dray horses – to drag Cartwright's car out of a ditch. "It was pretty common to get stuck," Scott grins, "but it seemed more common for Bert than for others."

"Would he have to walk far to get to your place?"

"All depends where he got stuck."

"Mile?"

"Yeah . . . but he didn't like to walk too far."

"I met him one time when he wanted to check the dam," says Skoropata. "He asked us to take his group out. There was a lot of water that year and we knew our way around," Skoropata says, pointing at Scott with a thumb. "In order to get in you had to know how to use the trails – where to cross over in shallow spots and where the ground was firm. We drove in only so far with a jeep. Then we walked. Everybody was peeling off their boots and socks to wade through. Cartwright, he said he couldn't wade bare feet. So he just walked the way he was, all the way out to the dam in his oxfords."

The first shift began hard work at the Duck Factory in 1939. A 42-foot steel lookout tower was erected, fencing built to check wandering cattle, and 27 miles of fireguard was turned.

Using borrowed workhorses or an antiquated Farmall, the early DUers turned over long sod furrows, stretching from one

Ducks Unlimited chief naturalist Bert Cartwright. Hired May 1, 1938, Cartwright held the position until his retirement in 1960.

end of Big Grass Marsh to the other. With the dirt exposed, theoretically, a running marsh fire would not be able to jump the plowed area. "It only worked on surface fires, and it was a terrible ordeal to plow," says Scott. "In places where you've got soil, it works, but not where there's peat. The peat can be four feet deep, there's no way to plow it." The fireguards required maintenance – frequent discing was needed to hold vegetation down.

Living onsite in the cabin, biologist Bob Harris was the project's first caretaker, and as such, was not pining for things to do. He checked dams and maintained water levels. He patrolled the marsh for poachers, made brood count surveys and fought fires. He built duck traps and banded birds. He collected and kept tidbits of information with the tenacity of a detective, reporting all of those weekly to Cartwright. Harris' cabin was jammed to the rafters with equipment including a pioneer cook stove, coffee and teapots, dishes and all manner of utensils, a 250-gallon cistern, two snowshoes, one canoe, one swede saw, one claw hammer, two stoplog

Local ranchers lend a hand, and equipment, to turn fireguard.

Flames frequently bit into the sod surrounding the marsh. Locals beat out the flames with tools and wet bags.

hooks. For reading material: *Birds of Canada, Hawks of North America, Food of Game Ducks,* and *Game Management* by Aldo Leopold, the 1933 bible of conservation followed by DU Canada.

Harris hiked. He made intensive nest searches. From these came the basis for his 1939 production estimate of 623 ducklings. He was disappointed in the dry conditions that led to the number, especially since Cartwright had estimated a large number of broods the year before, and aerial surveys had picked up 5,000 ducks on Jackfish Lake. Harris' weekly reports reflect hard work and drama. His June 3, 1940 report tells Cartwright of a conflagration in the marsh.

One of the worst fires of this year started up at about 6 p.m. on May 28 near the ditch just west of John Arnason's old dam. I reached it at 7 p.m., and at 10 o'clock received help from John Arnason and his two hired men. The fire, burning fiercely in a mass of old sedge and thatch grass, was very hard to beat out. By midnight we had made no progress whatever, and the north wing of the fire was gradually advancing toward Jackfish Lake ... as soon as the fire reached the phragmites on the bank of the ditch it traveled northward with amazing speed, the flames reaching to a height of 20 feet at times. It was now 3:30 and ... as no one seemed capable of working any longer without rest, I called it off for a few hours.

At 7:30 a.m. the fire was burning strongly again. ... I went to get the help of Scott and Goodmanson, and met the latter returning from the fire. He immediately phoned for Schneider to come out with his tractor to plough a fireguard ... by 2 o'clock a fireguard had been ploughed here and the whole northern side made safe. ... Another fireguard was made at the south side of the fire. ... The ploughing was finished at 10:30 with the aid of a lantern.

The municipality will pay half the cost of ploughing. In addition to the tractor, I hired six men for a total of 74½ hours. However, Arnason, Scott and Goodmanson have given half their time, which brings the total down to 55 hours.

"Years ago everybody was friendly with the Ducks Unlimted," says Skoropata. "Today, people don't want to do much for each other, but back then, anybody that came along, we would help."

"Our relations with the farmers and ranchers living around the project continue to be excellent," wrote Harris in his 1939 annual report. "Realizing that the marsh has been deteriorating into a burned-out desert, they unanimously

Pulling stoplogs, fighting fires,
snaring poachers and banding
ducks, Kenny Matthews served as
Big Grass caretaker from 1942 to
1945. "It was a job I enjoyed,"
he says. "I've always worked
outdoors."

approve of our efforts to restore the water level."

Work was no stranger to Scott and Skoropata, and neither was the idea of conservation. But the ranchers had never connected the two. Conservation was simply the local signs they saw designating Big Grass as a bird sanctuary. The idea of expending so much sweat on behalf of ducks was foreign. But following Harris' lead, they, too, began working their heads off.

Scott loaned saddle horses to early dam maintenance crews. Skoropata, in the forties and fifties, helped band geese. A pen was set up in his yard and Canadas were imported from the Delta Marsh by biologists in an effort to expand the bird's range. Both men helped drag stoplogs from the dams and fought fires. As prairie firemen, their expenses ran about $5 per day. They beat out flames with wet bags, plowed fireguard and handled "early burnings" – the springtime torching of grasses well before nesting. The early fires would take away the potential fuel source that could ignite when the fields were full of nests.

"We were cattlemen, and what the Ducks Unlimited was doing didn't appear to hurt us," says Scott. "They brought a little water in here for us. They didn't offer full-time employment to anyone around here . . . except Kenny Matthews. He watched the dams."

"Will he take us out to that cabin?" Code anxiously cuts in.

"No, Matthews lives down in Portage la Prairie now, but he would know all of this."

Far from Langruth, standing in his tiny backyard alongside a noisy Royal Canadian Air Force Base, Matthews is busy. Puffing a cigarette without benefit of filter, the bent-over 78-year-old looks concerned. About 30 rows of onions – three different varieties – beg thinning. Does Matthews like onions?

"I don't eat one-tenth of one percent of what's out here," he says. "I give the rest away. It's something to do. I've always worked outdoors." Wandering about the thick, green grass behind the old, white brick house, he inspects his four gardens and scratches his head as Fifi, his little white-and-brown puff dog, trails behind with quick, choppy steps. Ever alert, the wide-eyed sentinel never lets her roommate get too far away. Picking up his little dog, Matthews walks to the back porch. "I stay here now. I used to get around, worked all over. Still have my snowshoes that I used at Big Grass Marsh – Ojibways, 14 inches by 60 inches. Now Fifi is all the company I have."

Matthews' gypsy life led him across western Canada and to points beyond. Leaving his father's farm at 17, he switched jobs with the seasons, a barn-building carpenter in Saskatchewan during summers, a commercial fisherman on Lake Manitoba in winters. After rambling the summer long, he'd home in on Langruth to help his father gather the winter wood, then dash five miles east to Big Point, on the big lake.

The fishermen drove their teams seven miles out onto the ice, set up shacks and camped there. Cutting holes 80 yards

17

RETURN TO BIG GRASS

Big Ojibway snowshoes carried Matthews on patrol through the winter marsh. And when supplies were needed, the wood-and-gut frames were the only means to make it across six miles of prairie drifts to Langruth.

apart, they used ropes, poles and hooks to stretch their gill nets beneath the ice, later to haul up straining meshes of perch, pike, whitefish and tullibee. When the camps had accrued enough fish to make a good load, the fishermen piled their catches onto a wagon. Supplies could be expected back on the same wagon two days hence.

The life of a commercial fisherman was no softer than that of his cattle-and-sheep running neighbors during depression days. Matthews fished the winter, then dug herbs all summer long. "That was tough. I was married and had three boys. I dug senega roots for seven cents a pound, green."

In 1939, looking for better money, Matthews joined the Fourth Battalion of Engineers in the Canadian Army. The 32-year-old corporal was shipped to England as a paratrooper.

Three months in the hospital with a damaged knee was enough to convince army doctors that Matthews should be sent home. He was discharged September 24, 1942. And it wasn't too long after he got back to Manitoba, that Matthews fell into a job.

Water was flowing over the dams for the first time on Big Grass Marsh, and from that point on the wetland flourished. Young Harris had put up fence, supervised haying and patrolled for poachers. But that year, DU's biologist/ ranger/ caretaker/manager enlisted in the Royal Canadian Air Force. He moved out of the cabin and Matthews moved in.

As the first non-biological type Ducks Unlimited hired to look after Big Grass, Matthews had plenty to learn. But he was more than willing since his new position was his first real, honest-to-paycheck, year-round employment.

Now holding Fifi in his lap, browsing through *Ducks and Men*, DU Canada's fortieth anniversary book from 1978, he spots a picture of the cabin.

"I *liked* it there. That cabin was *nice*," he says, noting that he is not surprised the structure took less than a month to build since it was prefabricated. "Do you know they had cedar log siding on there? It was logs cut in half, tongue-in-grooved together. It fit so nice it looked like real logs. The corners were perfect 45s. It was all varnished. Oh, it was a pretty little building!" he smiles. "There was a little wood stove so it was a nice, warm little cabin. It had a big bedroom, a nice kitchen and a great big front room with a big window. I could set there and look outside whenever I pleased," he says, turning the page, then stopping short.

"Bert!"

Spotting his friend pictured in a pose before the cabin gate, Matthews stops paging, a big grin decorating his face. "Boy, this is interesting. I've never seen these pictures." Staring down, finger tracing the page, he scrutinizes the photo. "That's *my* gate!" That's the one I built! See?! See this cable? I fastened it up here so the gate wouldn't sag. Here comes my cable, see? Right down to the gate.

"I knew Bert Cartwright for an awful lotta years. He would come out, sometimes with his wife, sometimes alone. Used to stay a few days, maybe almost a week. Nobody knew his birds like Bert did."

Working alongside the naturalist with the bad stomach, Matthews learned a marshful of wildlife facts.

"One time it was all froze up, and we were snowshoeing across Jackfish Lake," Matthews remembers. "He spotted some jackrabbit tracks. Suddenly they stretched out, farther apart. 'What scared him?' Bert said. The tracks were heading toward the rushes. Then we saw it. Wingtip marks in the snow. It was a snowy owl, and the rabbit was beating it for the cover. What was left of the rabbit was frozen, right in front of the rushes. It was all written in the snow."

18

*Bert Cartwright and his pet project.
Cartwright visited Matthews and
neighbor John Arnason on a
regular basis despite a 100-mile
trip from Winnipeg on poor roads,
and even no roads at all.*

BIG GRASS MARSH DUCK FACTORY No.1
RESTORED AND MANAGED BY DUCKS UNLIMITED

19

Matthews scaling the 42-foot lookout tower. Built just west of the cabin in 1939, the steel frame provided the caretaker an observatory to spot fires and poachers.

When Cartwright wasn't able to come out to observe wildlife, he kept current on the rhythms of the marsh by relying on Matthews as his ears and eyes. The caretaker checked in by mail on a weekly basis. Matthews' assorted assignments included counting the ducks and estimating broods as well as watching the dams. An effective census taker, his letters reflect a lot of walking.

Langruth, Manitoba
May 19, 1943

Dear Bert:

Here is the rest of the duck count on Jackfish Lake: Mallard –50. Pintail–90. Teal–370. Shovelers–180. Scaup–600. Goldeneye–20. Red Heads–500. Cans–350. Ruddy ducks –300. Baldpate–80. Bufflehead–30.

Am going down to south dam tomorrow for two days, and take a count of ducks there . . . found two nests destroyed, one by sheep and the other by ground squirrels. They are very numerous. Could you please get me a permit to carry a .22 rifle as I could destroy quite a few crows and ground squirrels? I have caught 60 ground squirrels so far. . . . The north dam is leaking very bad. Seems to come up from the bottom. Must be fixed as soon as possible.

Yours Truly,
Ken Matthews

"I watched the dams like a hawk, but I never had to repair 'em, thank God," Matthews says. "That was a game preserve, but I had authority to take all the predators out of the marsh. The first year I took out 60 skunks. I got three coyotes, I forget how many mink I took out. There was no foxes up there, but I took part near a hundred weasel."

The scrappy-tough 160 pounder also spent time scouring the marsh for skunks of another sort. Guided by binoculared reconnaisance from the lookout tower, he hunted on foot, on horseback and by car, for poachers.

Reestablishment of the Big Grass ecosystem brought with it a resurgence in muskrat populations, and Cartwright hit on an idea. In an effort to give something back to the municipalities that had granted free leases to DU, and in one of the premier plans to illustrate the economic value of a marsh, he established the Big Grass Muskrat Management Ranch. Run by Matthews, and the caretakers after him, the ranch worked like this. The municipality, through the caretaker, would hire 40 trappers, generally from the Sandy Bay Tribe, or veterans out of work. Traps were supplied and each man given a zone to work. Muskrat skins were pooled and auctioned on the fur trading block in Winnipeg. The venture's largest take came in 1946, when some 16,000 rats brought nearly $52,000 to the trappers and municipality. DU took nothing.

Langruth, Manitoba
February 15, 1943

Dear Bert:

Well, we are snowbound up here. Snow up to your hips. There will be plenty of water to fill the marsh up this spring. I know most of the ducks but there are three or four I am not just sure of, so would be thankful for a little help on that this spring. . . . The muskrat houses have come through in wonderful shape. I've tested them all over the marsh. There should be a very good catch of them this spring . . .

With the Best of Luck,
Yours Sincerely,
K. Matthews

To ensure a good catch, the poachers had to be checked. "I patrolled on one of John Arnason's saddle horses 'til the snow

got too deep. Then it was snowshoes," Matthews says. Most poachers were illegally taking muskrat, but at least one was shooting ducks. "Old Charlie Fisher lived on the west side of the marsh. I had no boat and couldn't get across. He knew it too. He could slide his boat in and shoot and be out before I got anywhere near him," Matthews says. "One day I took my car to Gladstone and came up from the south. I worked my way through the reeds, back and forth, back and forth. It took me all day, but I finally found his boat. I burned it," he laughs.

"Later on I saw Charlie in the beer parlor in Langruth. We were friends, and he knew he had been doing wrong in the marsh. I says 'Charlie, you been buyin' any lumber lately?' 'No,' he says, 'what do I want lumber for?'

"I just smiled," Matthews says.

Though the line grew increasingly blurred over when and

how he worked for the municipality, Matthews still had plenty to do for DU. A big task was to trap and band ducks.

Langruth, Manitoba
August 4, 1943

Dear Bert:

Have been rather under the weather this week, my old knee is giving me plenty of grief. Have seven duck traps in operation. The young mallard and teal are showing up very good. Most of the sloughs east of the marsh are drying up and the ducks are pouring into the marsh quite heavy. . . . There are about 3,000 pintail, 1,500 mallard, 500 teal, 500 shovelers, 150 ruddy ducks, 200 red heads, 50 bald-pates and 50 green-winged teal from the south end of Jackfish Lake to the north dam. Some places there were 500 ducks to a loafing bar . . . will you please send me some more record sheets for ducks?

Yours Truly,
Ken

Astride neighbor John Arnason's saddle horse, Matthews is set for summer patrol. The 30-30 rifle was for animal predators—not poachers.

BIG GRASS MARSH DUCK FACTORY Nº1
RESTORED AND MANAGED BY DUCKS UNLIMITED

"Oh, yes, Bert taught me to band. You use a little, round pliers. Different size ducks take different size bands—but I never had enough of them," Matthews complains. "I had a bunch of big traps going and I was catching ducks by the hundreds. I'd phone in and Bert would send me out a hundred bands. Maybe two, three days later, I'd need more so I'd call. He'd only send another hundred. I finally called and said 'Listen, Bert, don't be cheap—*send me some bands, dammit.*' He sent a hundred. I was getting mad. I made him come out here. When we were working, he said 'Yup, now I see why you need so many,' but he was smiling when he said it. Sent 500 after that."

A diligent record keeper, Matthews kept data on all his

DU biologists began banding ducks at Big Grass Marsh in 1939. Later, Canada geese from Delta Marsh were banded and released at the DU project in an effort to expand the bird's range.

where it was, and the time. It was as interesting as could be. Like getting a letter." By 1945, when Matthews left Big Grass, DU Canada had erected 165 projects encompassing 1,263,200 acres. Over 42,000 ducks had been banded on the projects.

Today the Canadian Wildlife Service runs banding operations on Big Grass Marsh, giving birds anklets from the third week in July through the first week in September. According to the CWS, Big Grass Marsh sends most of its ducks on a southeasterly swing through the Mississippi Flyway. But pintails banded there have turned up in California, and other waterfowl were recovered a continent away from Duck Factory Number One. The blue-winged teal are the travelers of the bunch. One banded in August 1978, got to Gorgona, Panama. Another, banded in August 1975, was taken in Laguna la Deseada, Mexico. Still another, banded the same month, ended up in Merritt Island, Florida. Hovey Lake, Indiana; Monticello, Florida; Greenville, Missouri; Mayersville, Mississippi; and Morris, Oklahoma, are only a handful of the huge list of localities, both provincial and state, benefitted by Big Grass birds.

Even with his great interest in the banding project, Kenny Matthews says it was not enough to hold him in the cozy cabin beyond 1945. He quit, headed for DU dam building projects on the Pipestone River in south Saskatchewan.

"I didn't quit DU, oh no! I just quit that rat business. DU had nothin' to do with the fur atall," Matthews says.

The Matthews/municipality rift really began to stink as time went by. It seems that a light-colored rat pelt brought more money than a dark one. In order to achieve a lighter color, special care was required during the drying process. The skins had to be dried slowly, out of the sun.

"The municipality wouldn't give me my goddam drying

banded ducks, a copy for himself, one for the U.S. Fish and Wildlife Service and one for DU Canada. "Well, I got returns from all over the states, South America, Alaska. And interesting?! Oh, man! I got the person's name who shot it,

Powered with a Model B Ford engine, Everett Schneider's snowplane would wind up to 40 miles per hour under proper conditions. "It was a real wild ride," says Schneider. "You could jump cracks in the ice easily." Schneider lived at the Big Grass cabin from 1946 through 1954 and used his snowplane on patrol.

Everett Schneider (left), George Scott and Pete Skoropata at the north dam on Big Grass Marsh.

shed, so I was drying 'em in my house," Matthews snorts, with an embarrassed look. "Hundreds of pelts, and the municipality wouldn't give it to me," he says, getting more agitated with each word. "A *tannery* that's what it smelled like! Well, I'm not gonna lay on top of them smelly, dirty hides... well... not dirty, but all them hides *did* smell."

Leaving for Saskatchewan, Matthews talked his older brother Gordon into taking the job. Gordon lasted a year before Everett Schneider took over as caretaker in 1946.

"I got out of the army in January 1946. Wanted to trap and didn't know nothing about it," Schneider says. "Gordon handed me a bundle of traps and said, 'Go at it.'"

Schneider has barely joined his neighbors Scott and Skoropata in the Langruth Cafe, when Gass, the itchy mountie, beats both Code and I to the punch.

"Where was that cabin?"

Rather than telling the story, the ranchers decide, they will show us... with all this help, might we find a fort today?

Exiting the cafe into the bright sun on the wide Langruth street, Scott, Schneider and Skoropata pack themselves into Gass' Bronco. Cabin hunting we will go.

Spinning west over crunchy gravel roads, boring into the burnt orange of a clear Manitoba afternoon, our little group has six bumpy miles to make before reaching the spot.

By the time Schneider had taken over the caretaker's duties in 1946, DU had grown prodigiously. In just eight years, annual income from the states stood at $428,675, generated by nearly 25,000 members. The 165 projects that had been carried out, including three built by Matthews in Saskatchewan, needed attention. And so did all the proposed projects ramrodded by Tommy Main. By 1950, with a small staff and 307 projects on line, a resident manager was a luxury for any single DU project. Thus came the concept of the

"Project Manager" – one traveling supervisor to keep an eye on 20 to 25 projects in a region.

Not only had DU's project inventory grown, it was spreading. Though Big Grass Marsh was a very large project, it certainly was not DU's only project, and as such, could no longer have so much attention lavished upon it. The water was there, the marsh was secure, and other wetlands needed saving. But the project itself was not neglected.

Riding shotgun, directing Gass down dusty gravel roads, Scott looks across the green fields. "Back when we worked for the Ducks Unlimited we did all our work with horses – horses were the standby. You could depend on those. The horses we used to have, they were not the horses you see now. I haven't seen a nice horse in about 15 years." Scott grumps, looking across passing pastures. "We had heavier horses. We had *workhorses*. Belgians, perchins and clydes, but mostly perchins."

Percherons?

"Yeah, perchins. Boy we had some beautiful horses in here. Soon as they had no use for 'em anymore they started raisin' these, whatchacallem... *quarter horses*."

Scott with his gray team of percherons, and Skoropata with his strawberry roan Belgians, could outpull anyone, they say, and still have enough left over to yank Cartwright's car from the ditch.

"Stop here," Scott commands, and the Bronco pulls in front of a gray, fallen-in farmstead, just one mile from the lane that Code, Mindy and I had hunted cabins on the evening before. "This is my place – where those cabin builders stayed."

Rail fences and a few weathered buildings stand scattered around the grounds, shingle-sided shacks gnawed apart by ruminating cattle. The old Sandy Bay Trail lightly traces a

line through the dusty front yard.

Skoropata leads the way onto the adjacent farm, now a graveyard for old shacks and buildings that have been moved there. He lifts a fence gate. "Here's the original bank of Langruth," he laughs, pointing to a structure that might pass for an outsized outhouse. "And Everett, you recognize these."

Schneider wanders over to a slant-roofed shed and a 16-foot by 16-foot garage. "These were at the cabin site," he nods, looking at the paint-peeled structures. The drying shed and utility building that Matthews quit over were finally constructed by the municipality in the 1950s. By the 1970s they were sold and carted to where they now sit. The cabin was sold then too, and was finally moved north where it stands along the west shore of Lake Manitoba.

Climbing back into the Bronco, Gass looks itchy. It will not be long now, as he four-wheels it through grassy fields.

"Here's John Arnason's," Scott says. "Turn here."

"This is where the DU guys had to drive in to get to their place," Skoropata adds. "Be careful, there's no real roads anywhere in here." Bumping and bouncing down dual-rutted grassy paths, the four-wheeler halts at the same brush patch Code and I had found.

The old Langruth ranchers have not visited the site in nearly 30 years. It was 1956 when they quit their DU duties here. Like boy scouts, Scott, Schneider and Skoropata bust from the Bronco to survey the scene.

Stepping across telltale, overgrown ruts, Schneider points at the ground. "Here's your fireguard you were talking about. This is a double one, ten rods wide. They made a big one cause there were buildings here, eh?"

Already kneeling at Code's concrete pad, Scott and Skoropata wait for Schneider to catch up. "No, the cabin wasn't here," Scott says. "This was the garage... when did that go in

Everett?"

"Early 1950s, I guess. We kept the traps and stretchers in it. The cabin sat over there."

Staring down at the broken concrete chunks – a straight piece, and another, and a foundation corner – Skoropata points to the ruins of the cabin's base. "*Here's* where it was... and don't step there," he warns, pointing out the grown-over shaft sunk deep into the ground. "The cistern... they collected rainwater in there."

One lone fencepost stands at the edge of the brushy yard, a sentinel in the waves of blowing grasses, still straight, aged gracefully in gray. It is all that is left here, in the spot where Kenny Matthews' gate once swung, and where a big sign, tall and proud, once stood up to tell the world that, damn right, this is Duck Factory Number One. Pieces of concrete in the prairie grass are all that bear witness to the brutal work done by so many men, so long ago. But while the ranger's cabin may be gone, the hard work and spirit of Ducks Unlimited remain.

To the west, a pair of strong, concrete dams guard the marsh. The very ditches that killed Big Grass now belong to broods of teal and mallards. More important than managers and cabins and muskrat hides and, yes, even a drying shed, is this legacy.

Big Grass Marsh stands for a new conservation ethic. Big Grass Marsh stands as a warning against man's greed and folly. And Big Grass Marsh stands today, more than anything else, as a monument to hard-working men like Joseph P. Knapp, men who thought differently, men who wanted to put something back.

The Grass Fort? The Duck Fort? Standing at the lonesome fencepost, I felt as though this fort should have a name... but someone had already done it for me a long, long time ago.

DU COUNTRY

I compiled most of the journalistic material for this section during trips I made between May and October of 1985. My hope was to share with *Big Grass* readers not only some of the geographic diversity of Ducks Unlimited's wetland projects, but the degree to which their very design and construction is dictated by the kinds of terrain in which they exist. Though I knew, for instance, that DU's prairie projects were built to withstand the long-term effects of drought, I did not know that biologists and engineers in mountain country often have to deal with a surplus of water precisely at those times when they least want it. Or that DU Canada's coastal efforts, in the Maritimes, are geared to contending with the tidal fluctuations of the sea.

Every bit as interesting as the contrast in DU's regional wetland programs is the variety of flora and fauna found in each. Managing Editor Nicoletta Barrie reviewed over 7,000 pictures solicited from some of the country's finest free-lance wildlife photographers. After more than a year of ongoing, meticulous editing she narrowed the submissions to less than 100, then began the seemingly never-ending process of shaping the final selection of photographs to my text. The result is a collection of "DU Country" visuals which are a good bet to be some of the most memorable wildlife photos you have seen in a long time.

One note about the material in the Mexico section—it was gathered during a trip I made to inspect Ducks Unlimited de Mexico projects in the spring of 1983. Since then this unique program has grown considerably. There are now 46 active wetland projects in Mexico boasting nearly 80,000 acres. The work ranges from the desert country of the state of Coahuila to the rain forest of Quintana Roo. —*RW*

Mountain

It was nearly nine o'clock on a Tuesday morning in early April when Frank Hogan noticed the fog was beginning to lift around the narrow truss bridge over the Bull River. He had parked his highway department pickup off the shoulder of the graveled road shortly after eight. The morning was a cold one, and Frank had been content to sit in the truck with the heater fan on low while he sipped coffee, ate two chocolate-coated doughnuts and paged his way slowly through the local Cranbrook paper. With the fog swirling heavy around the truck Hogan could barely make out the bridge let alone begin work on it. An annual inspection two weeks before had revealed minor deterioration of several trusses. Hogan had figured on checking the trusses over this morning and making what repairs he could before returning to his regional headquarters for a meeting that afternoon. There was actually no big push on the work. Most of the traffic along these roads winding high into the Steeple Range of the Rockies in the Kootenay region of southeast British Columbia would come with the summer tourist season. But Hogan liked the idea of showing up at the meeting having put in a solid half day of work on the bridge.

He had not been out of the truck for five minutes before he saw the bear—a huge, dark grizzly moving down the hill along the side of the road toward the river where Hogan stood drinking coffee on the bridge. The bear was not moving quickly, nor did it ever appear to look at him, but the fact that it was only 40-odd yards up the hill and getting closer froze Hogan tight.

With his stomach all hollow feeling and his legs seeming not part of him at all, he carefully began stepping backwards toward the truck. Fighting a heart-pounding impulse to turn and run, Hogan never took his eyes off the bear. Its massive head swung from side to side as it continued down the hill toward the bridge in a lumbering, sweeping motion which

Ursus arctos horribilis, *the grizzly bear, is not so much a fiend as it is an animal who prefers to be left alone. Taken by surprise, however, the bruin will not hesitate to attack. Grizzlies are no strangers to British Columbia's Kootenay region where DU began work in 1969.*

covered an area between the shoulder of the road and the edge of the woods. When Hogan suddenly bumped into the grille of the pickup, what remained of his coffee splashed down his khaki pants. Sliding ever so slowly around the front fender and opening the door at last to the safety of the cab triggered a sigh deep within him. For several long moments he simply sat behind the wheel of the truck listening to the rush of the river. The bear had disappeared into the big timber, but for now Hogan was not eager to resume work on the bridge.

"Depending on the wind, that bear likely didn't know the guy was even there," said Lloyd Jones. "Point is, he couldn't have cared less about him. The bear might have come in and out of the Doug fir looking for a road kill, just passing the morning, or he may have thought about using the bridge to cross the river before heading into the high country to check out a snowslide in the afternoon.

"This time of year they'll do that, you know, attracted by a goat or a sheep or a deer that got caught in one of last winter's avalanches. They'll keep digging at that frozen slide 'til the afternoon sun melts off the ice to where the bear can get at what he wants to eat. I've seen them scratch and paw around a place, then slide up and down that avalanche four or five times just for the hell of it."

Dave Klassen and I were listening to Lloyd while we stood on the bridge where one month earlier Hogan had backpedaled to his pickup. It was seven o'clock, with the sun still high, on a clear, cool, wonderful-smelling May mountain evening. I'd spent the day with Dave who is Ducks Unlimited Canada's area manager out of the Creston office. He'd introduced me earlier to Lloyd, a local rancher, who has returned to British Columbia after 30 years of big game outfitting in the States. Much of Lloyd's time now is devoted to managing his Top of the World guest ranch. He is a man who knows something about grizzlies, and had been eager to share the story of the bear on the bridge.

"How big would a bear like that run?" I asked Lloyd. Pale, spring sunlight sifted down through several of the large ponderosa and lodgepole pines lining the river gorge, and suddenly I felt tingly all over thinking about where Hogan's grizzly might be on a night like tonight.

"Lots of people will talk about a griz weighing 800, maybe 900 pounds," said Lloyd, "but that's stretching it a bit. A big

The dike and interlocking project segments of Bummers Marsh provide ducks and geese with stabilized water levels even through spring snowmelt. Without DU controls, the Kootenay River would flood the wetland during nesting season.

grizzly is 600 to 700 pounds. That's a big animal – there's damned few black bear that'll weigh 500. Under average conditions, they claim a grizzly will weigh 100 pounds for every inch of his front foot's width. A bear whose track measures seven inches across will be in the range of 700 pounds. The grizzly hanging around this bridge, mind you, could not have been out of its den very long. His weight might have been down to 400, but come fall, with good feed, he could go 650. It depends on what kind of a year we have for berries and whatnot. With warmer weather that bear will graze like a horse over early exposures looking for wild onions, pine grass, balsam root and Saskatoon berries. Hell, he'll jerk the bark right off a white pine and eat the cambium layer."

"So he doesn't mess generally with people?" I asked. Klassen and I had been listening to Lloyd with the spellbound attentiveness of young children. Outside of the roar of the Bull River, there was nothing else save the sound of crunching gravel. Throughout our bear conversation Dave had taken to stirring some around by the bridge railing underneath his boot.

"There's no guarantee," said Lloyd. "But a grizzly basically has very little interest in people. Hunting him, though, is a different piece of business. I remember a guide right here in the Steeples two seasons back, the year after we returned from the States. His hunter wounded a big griz late in the evening, and in the morning, when they went looking for him, *he* came looking for them. Caught the guide and chewed up the upper part of his body, all up over his shoulders, his head and one side of his face."

"Did the bear kill him?" asked Dave.

"Didn't kill him," answered Lloyd, "but he overhauled him pretty good." Dave began crunching on a fresh batch of gravel and I suspected that he may have been trying to imagine, as was I, what someone actually looks like once a grizzly has removed a major portion of his face. "Another thing," said Lloyd reaching into the pocket of his faded blue, lightly insulated zipper jacket from which he pulled a piece of gum. "If another animal, or a person, stumbles on a grizzly and spooks him, you can bet he'll charge you. There's no doubt about that. He'll come right up, stand up and woof at you. But something people don't know is that if you stand your ground and holler at him, 90 percent of the time that bear will back off." Lloyd peeled the wrapper off his gum and looked at me. "Course," he said, "there's not many fellas that will do that.

"We best begin moving into high country," Lloyd said staring down the road toward where Dave had parked his

Ford Bronco. "Game will start coming out around eight, so the Yank here can get his look at elk and some other animals then."

It was 43 degrees with mare's tails spiraled high in the sky to the north and west of Cranbrook, British Columbia, when Klassen met me at the airport early that morning. My flight across the Rockies from Calgary, Alberta, had featured good visibility so the cloud formation above Cranbrook was my first clue that bad incoming weather might make for a rainy look at two Ducks Unlimited wetland projects here in the Kootenays. What had interested me with what I'd heard about this piece of DU country was the fact that too much water, as opposed to

Ten tundra swans take time out for a rest on DU's Bummers Marsh before continuing on their long journey to arctic nesting grounds.

Though it migrates in flocks, the common snipe is by nature a secretive marsh bird. It can often be found feeding alone at dusk or dawn along the water's edge.

On a still-chilly spring morning, newly bloomed violet and white phlox are covered with frost. Phlox diffusa is but one of 60 species of this flower found throughout Canada, Mexico and all 50 states.

Were it not for the white ring around their bills, these ring-necked ducks would blend in with shoreline cover just fine. The bird, oddly enough, derived its name not from its decorative bill, but from the barely discernible ring around its neck.

too precious little, routinely poses waterfowl management problems. Spring mountain snowmelt could be counted on more often than not to flood regional marshes at a time when newly returned ducks and geese are in the market for homes offering the kind of stable water levels which make for secure nesting sites.

"It's what we classify as a floodplain marsh," said Dave as we left the town of Cranbrook behind us and headed northeast on highway 95 toward Fort Steele. "Our control structures are geared as much to keeping water out at this time of year as they are to keeping water in. You'll get a feel for what I mean up at Bummers Marsh," he said pointing his finger casually toward the Bronco's windshield which was just now beginning to be splattered with a soft spring rain. "The marsh stretches right along the Kootenay River in what's known as the Rocky Mountain Trench. It'll be the Purcell Mountains you'll be seeing off to the west, with the main range of the Rockies up behind you to the east."

We were 60 some miles north of the Idaho/Montana border and a long way from Big Grass Marsh. But since Ducks Unlimited operations began in British Columbia back in 1969 the construction program has mushroomed, I learned, to a point that 252 projects now thread through the province. "We don't have the project stats that those stubble jumpers have over on the prairies," said Dave with an easy, relaxed laugh. "We're gaining on them though, and the 22 projects we've built through the Kootenay region are located in country which involves some pretty rough stuff."

In addition to being rough, the country is not shy on overall size. The East and West Kootenays include a total acreage larger than the combined area of Massachusetts, Vermont, New Hampshire and Rhode Island. The Kootenai Indians, Dave pointed out, once roamed this land. Numbering about

1,200 in the late eighteenth century, the tribe was divided into upper and lower divisions. Today, the Lower Kootenai Band is headquartered on a reserve in Creston, and Dave made it clear that the Indians have been hard-nosed supporters of Ducks Unlimited. Interesting, also, was what he told me about the tribal hierarchy. In addition to a top-dog chief and a war chief, the Kootenai appointed a chief of fish, a chief of deer and a chief of ducks.

The drizzle had petered out by the time Dave swung off 95 onto the shoulder which dropped sharply to a set of railroad tracks. We each got out of the vehicle slowly, taking pains not to slam any doors, and with field glasses started down the gravel bank and across the tracks to a slope of an evergreened hill which overlooks Bummers Marsh. Bummers Flats is what the area itself is actually called – a name which dates back to the gold rush days of the 1860s when someone with no small amount of imagination decided to pack his grubstake on

DU COUNTRY

Before DU began its flood-control program on Bummers Marsh, nesting opportunities for Canada geese were few. Today some 60 nests dot the project acreage—a far cry from seasons past when the total counted by biologists was two.

camels. One of them, whose name was Bummer, was ultimately turned loose to forage on the river flats.

Though Bummer was not present today, 10 tundra swans were. Bunched in a quiltlike pattern next to a DU-constructed nesting island, they drifted about gracefully less than 50 yards offshore. The sun had broken through a wispy-thin cloud cover, and the murmuring sounds of the big white birds hung in the morning stillness with that haunting feel which to me is so much a part of the call of a mourning dove. Patches of purple and white phlox spread beneath our feet as Dave and I moved farther down the hill toward the water's edge. Suddenly, high above us, came the delicate, winnowing hum of a snipe courtship flight. Clearly somewhere along the line Bummers Marsh had cut itself a five-star rating with both local and migratory wildlife.

As we prowled the project together, Dave told me that before DU began work on Bummers in 1973 the spring flood water often backed up right across the flats onto the hill by the railroad tracks. What now prevents this from happening is a heavyweight stretch of dike which the British Columbia DU crew designed and built, a dike which provides the structural beef needed to keep the Kootenay River out when snowmelt peaks. There is a South and a Middle Bummers—two projects involving 353 acres, some 13 miles of shoreline and five control structures regulating water levels within the projects' four segments. A third project, North Bummers, will be completed in 1987. Meanwhile the whole affair, as Dave described it, works something like this.

Built by a cat and scraper using standard roadway fill, the 12-foot-high exterior dike manhandles the Kootenay floodwaters each year somewhere between the tenth and twentieth of June. During this period, water within the project is maintained at levels desirable to nesting waterfowl. When

the Kootenay waters recede and center stage becomes occupied by a hot summer sun, a 15-horsepower submersible pump moves water out of the river and into a holding pond where it flows in turn by gravity to the interior segments of the two projects. Thanks to the water level stabilization, Canada geese, mallards, teal, wigeon and ring-necked ducks now successfully nest on Bummers during snowmelt. And birds continue to utilize the marsh throughout the summer, when in years past the flow from local Saugum Creek could not be counted on to provide the water needed to see broods through.

A train whistle wails loud and long behind us, and the tundra swans rise up and over the pale green cottonwoods which stretch along Bummers' exterior dike on the river. Dave and I watch them and listen to their fading cries as they push north and then west against the snow-covered Purcells toward their faraway arctic nesting grounds. The train, Dave says, is headed west, likely toting coal to Robert's Bank where it will

As autumn's cool air comes to mountain country, the elk's velvety textured, stumpy summer rack spreads into bone-hard, glistening spines. Should you ever hear the whistling bugle of a herd bull, you will have heard something special. It is a sound you will not quickly forget.

during mid-June's flood season conditions are apt to look different from what I've seen today.

"I sure hope not," Dave replied. "If things are working as they're supposed to, water levels on Bummers then ought to be the same as what you're looking at right now."

Driving northeast on gravel out of Wasa Lake I smell the heavy, big-woods smell of ponderosa pine as we head up into the Rockies toward Premier Ridge and DU's Wolf Creek project. Bighorn sheep, elk, mule and white-tailed deer concentrate in this area come snow season making it one of the most important big game wintering ranges in British Columbia. Dave points out a monstrous looking six-foot by eight-foot multiplate culvert as the road swings sharply to the right. "You get the picture I guess, eh," he said. Through the culvert trickled Wolf Creek – a stream whose depth looked at best to be barely above a knee. "Come back with me to *this* place in flood season," Dave said, "and I'll show you a different looking Wolf Creek."

DU's Wolf Creek operation was constructed in 1981 and 1982 and is what Dave refers to as "a typical mountain stream runoff project." It consists of an upper and lower segment (9.4 and 26 acres respectively) offering waterfowl some two miles of nesting shoreline – shoreline whose water levels had varied so greatly, due to beaver activity and spring runoff, that ducks and geese could look to the mountain marsh for little more than a pitch-in-and-out resting spot during migration. But today the controls on the DU project's upper and lower sections keep the marsh's water level fluctuation within one foot even through flood season. The resulting improvements in water/cover interspersion have made for some quality territorial, nesting and loafing sites.

All of this is not to say that the beaver on Wolf Creek are out of the picture. As we stand on a catwalk at the dam on

A Caterpillar excavator trims up a section of interior dike on Bummers.

be shipped to the Japanese. The whistle blows again and spooks a small flock of cinnamon teal and four Canada geese, all of which swing wide across Middle Bummers before flaring south. "Can you believe only two goose nests here on the marsh before we began island construction," said Dave. "By 1982, we were routinely counting over 60."

It is nearly 11:30 a.m. and Dave has decided we'd best push on to Wolf Creek, a small DU project located in the Rockies northeast of the little town of Wasa Lake. As we climb back up the phlox-covered hill I turn to once again look out across Bummers. With the flat midday sun there is now sharp definition between the project segments giving the marsh from up here the feel of a carefully carved water mosaic. Off to the north I spot a piece of heavy construction equipment I hadn't noticed before. "That's contract work," said Dave, "a Caterpillar excavator trimming up a section of interior dike we never got to last season." And then, without first thinking, I idly remark that should I sometime return

DU COUNTRY

Come snowmelt, Wolf Creek's heavy flow will give this DU water-control structure all it can handle. The project is designed to keep the fluctuation of the marsh's water level within one foot.

A bald eagle may nest on the ground or in cliffs, but only when trees aren't available. Given their druthers, eagles opt for the highest branches of the tallest trees in places like this tamarack forest. Once they establish a nesting site, they return to it year after year. Nests weighing as much as a thousand pounds are the result of the annual addition of weeds and sticks.

Lower Wolf Creek, Dave stares down at some brushed-up aspen tucked tight around the bottom of a half-round stoplog water-control structure. "The beaver's main object in life," says Dave philosophically with a sad shake of his head, "is to stop the flow of water. I have seen them replace a dam two feet deep and 30 feet across overnight." There is a very light wind and the surface of the marsh shimmers as I look through the bright clear water at milfoils and sago pondweed.

"I wonder what would happen," I ask, "if I took a fly rod and cast a Mickey Finn out toward that bunch of bulrush?" Dave turned to me with a grin. "I can tell you from experience," said Dave, "that before too long you'd be tied up

with a native brookie."

Dave designed the Wolf Creek project and explained that the baffles on the fishway were constructed lower than the dam's two one-meter culvert pipes in order to attract brook, rainbow and cutthroat trout moving up and down the stream from the Kootenay. For those fish choosing not to use Klassen's ladder, the Creston DU crew carefully stretched fine textile material across the bottom of the pool below the dam. On top of it biologists spread a clean aggregate spawning bed material which helps reduce siltation during periods of heavy runoff.

Any threat of bad weather had long since disappeared. I looked out across the uplands sweeping up from the marsh and watched the light budding green colors of the birch, willow and aspen slowly turn deep green with the higher stands of pines, tamaracks and Douglas fir. White cumulus clouds drifted and puffed around the high peaks of the Rockies — peaks which Dave had said earlier may not be quite 10,000 feet "but are bumpin' on it." When I turned to Dave I realized he had started off toward the Bronco.

"You getting hungry?" he called back to me. It did not take me long to follow.

On the way to the Wasa Country Pub I asked Dave something that had been bugging me for over an hour. I asked him if maybe he wasn't starting to get awfully warm in his sheepskin vest. Anyone who'd been as cold in his life as much as he'd been, he replied, would just as soon stay warm for a little while so long as he had the chance.

Klassen's parents immigrated to Manitoba from Russia in 1926, and moved on to British Columbia in 1942. He grew up "down in the lower mainland," around the Vancouver area, and left high school in 1951 for a logging job "before he knew any better." Various sawmill operations took him from the

34

Four mule deer head toward evening water in the bottomlands. Two are adults, and two, young females. Young male fawns leave their mother the first year while females may stay for up to two.

"The beaver's main object in life," says Dave Klassen, DU Canada's area manager in Creston, British Columbia, "is to stop the flow of water." Before DU's Wolf Creek project, beaver activity and spring runoff prevented the mountain marsh from being little more than a resting spot during migration. Here, the creature's tail makes a splash on the water.

lower mainland into interior British Columbia. But after marrying a girl from Williams Lake, up in the Chilcotin region, he returned to Vancouver, finished high school, then went on to complete a year of work at the university level along with two years of technical school.

"My wife is a school teacher," said Dave, "and she's the one who paid the bills. I was never really unhappy with logging. But with the growing environmental concerns and what have you I developed an increased awareness and became what I guess you'd call uncomfortable."

Dave moved to Creston, in the Kootenays, in 1960. After working as a legal land surveyor with the Department of Highways, he joined Ducks Unlimited Canada in 1981. He and his family live on five acres of land outside of town in a log cabin which he built himself out of larch. Spring comes earlier to the Creston Valley, he told me, than it does to Cranbrook and this neck of the woods. "At this time of year, in early May, I can plant my peas and onion sets," Dave said. "But you don't plant the rest of the garden 'til you see the snow off the mountains."

"Pull over here!" said Lloyd Jones.
It was 8:20 p.m. and the three of us had long ago left the

Bull River bridge and climbed high in Dave's Bronco into the Steeple Range. Dave and Lloyd had gotten deep into the business basics of Ducks Unlimited Canada's work at Bummers Flats. What Dave had been pointing out to Lloyd was that DU had no interest in acquiring the acreage. It was owned by the province and managed on a day-to-day basis by the Fish and Wildlife Branch of the Ministry of Environment. So long as DU had a handle on a 30-year lease, its water-control program could be carried out just fine. As a rancher, Lloyd could meanwhile go about arranging grazing rights on a project like Bummers Marsh much like he would routinely do up in the high country on forestry administered Crown land. But once we had rounded this particular curve in the road and hit the brakes, all talk about leasing and cow/calf units was caught up short.

It was the first big game we had seen this evening: 18 bighorn sheep grazing undisturbed along the edge of a meadow. "Mainly ewes and little ones," said Lloyd, "but see there, off to the right, two young rams." I had barely focused field glasses on the sheep when Lloyd gave my shoulder a squeeze. "Mule deer," he said, "four of them down there in the bottom. They're moving toward water after feeding on that bunch of red-osier dogwood late this afternoon."

Up until this point in my life the only Rocky Mountain big game I had laid eyes on was the head of a stuffed elk which loomed above me as I ate chili in the Wasa Country Pub. A brass plaque noted that the elk had been shot by Ray Carric in 1979 with a .340 Weatherby, and that the animal had received a Boone and Crockett rating of 355.5. This, I came to find out later, translates into one hell of a lot of elk, but the impact was a minor one compared to the sheer joy I felt in watching the sheep and mule deer moving slowly in the spring evening light.

Prairie

The prairie country covers a vast amount of land, but 50 years ago it was where DU founders headed to make sure that droughts like the Dust Bowl thirties would never decimate North America's waterfowl again.

On June 8, 1985, a fast-moving front swept across southwestern Manitoba bringing with it a wind the likes of which prairie farmers had not seen for a long time. Lawrence Kelly remembers that day – remembers how he watched the storm from the safety of his home outside the town of Brandon. Had it not been the weekend, chances were good that on a routine workday he would have been caught driving along some stretch of gravel road out in the country where the wind howled through freshly planted fields of flax and canola. At times it blew in excess of 80 miles per hour, and Kelly is quick to point out that weather packing this kind of punch ought not to be observed from the cab of a pickup.

"There is a house across the road from where we live out in the country," says Kelly, "a house that is 500 to 600 feet away from us at most. Many times that afternoon we couldn't see that house. The clouds of dust kicked up by the wind kept on blowing right into evening. Our neighbor's field to the west was planted in canola seed and it was ripped out completely, topsoil and all. The dirt left underneath was packed hard as pavement. The next day most of the farm kids couldn't believe what they saw.

"There was never any rain, mind you, no hail, no thunder. Just the kind of wind that brought to mind the Dirty Thirties. The kind of hard times younger kids farming today don't know much about."

Kelly and I go back. He had helped me with a film production that was shot in the Brandon area for Ducks Unlimited shortly after I joined DU's Chicago staff in 1976. It was Kelly, DU Canada's land negotiator out of the area office, who had first shared with me some of the hydrology ABC's involved in DU's prairie projects. So it was naturally Kelly who came to mind when nearly 10 years later I was in need of a

Spring water conditions across the prairie pothole region dictate whether waterfowl will experience successful nesting seasons or not. If water becomes scarce, nearly 3,000 DU wetland projects do make a difference when ducks, geese and a host of other wildlife species seek refuge from drought.

At the extreme west end of Victoria Avenue in Brandon stood the remains of the glass Royal Oak Inn sign, broken up by a summer windstorm.

suggestion or two regarding material for the "prairie" section of DU's fiftieth anniversary book. I had told him over the phone that I had already taken a look at projects designed to keep out floodwaters during the spring snowmelt in mountain country far to the west. What I wanted to do now, I explained, was to find a prairie project whose primary objective was to hold water during periods of drought.

Kelly said he could provide the project, and that he could also provide the drought. Though I knew dry conditions across the prairies had made for tough waterfowl nesting through the early 1980s, I was not fully aware until I talked with him how critical the drought situation had become. In the spring of 1979, for example, there were some 792,000 "semipermanent" natural ponds in southern Manitoba – a number which biologists considered to be an average year. But by 1980 the number had been reduced to 286,000; in 1981, the May pond count slid to a 262,000 low. When you consider that the average tally between 1971 and 1980 stands at 841,000, and that a wet year such as 1974 produced 1,450,000 ponds, you can begin to imagine the impact that terribly dry back-to-back nesting seasons can have on the waterfowl resource. Since 1981, matters had gotten worse. "You come on up to Brandon," Kelly had said on the phone. "We'll show you the Alexander Griswold Marsh, and you'll see a DU prairie project that's earning its keep."

The update Kelly had given me late in June on the drought had produced information I'd written down for my Manitoba trip. The story he had related about the windstorm, however, seemed not to have traveled to Canada with me at all. Or perhaps I'd forgotten what he'd said at some point during the 130 miles I drove from Winnipeg to Brandon in the July heat. It was early afternoon on a Monday and I could not for the life of me find the Royal Oak Inn. I'd been told when making room

reservations that it was located in the west end of Brandon on Victoria Avenue, and it seemed to me right now that I was running out of west end and Victoria Avenue both. Then I noticed a sign in front of a car dealership was twisted into the shape of a pretzel. A bit farther on I passed a Burger King. It, along with an adjacent K-Mart, was minus any sort of street sign. Finally, I remembered Kelly's windstorm. Swinging the car around I found the motel, blown-out sign and all, nearly a mile behind me on the right.

After swimming fifteen minutes worth of mini-laps in the Royal Oak's pool I settled down with iced tea to some material which had been sent to me by Brandon area biologist Rick Andrews, whom I planned on seeing later this afternoon. The summary of DU's prairie program generally and Alexander Griswold Marsh specifically was all good background stuff, but it struck me as I read through it that the details would be particularly spellbinding to those early DU leaders who set

Come September, the long, lazy days of summer on the Canadian prairies draw to a close. There is a fresh feel to the wind, and a bright, sparkling expanse of sky. No one has to tell the Canada geese that another nesting season is over. It's time to move out and head toward the wintering grounds.

the stage for the construction of Big Grass Marsh. Today, nearly 50 years after its completion, 1,971 DU wetland projects stretch across the prairie provinces of Manitoba, Saskatchewan and Alberta – a network representing some 70 percent of DU's total Canadian work to date. At 2,650 acres Alexander Griswold Marsh helps anchor the effort to minimize the repercussions of drought in southwestern Manitoba. Built with funds from the Illinois Department of Conservation, it is located only 75 miles from its Big Grass

sister flagship which fights the drought to the northeast.

Before Ducks Unlimited implemented its construction program on the Alexander Marsh in 1978 and 1979, the residents of the little farming towns of Alexander (nestled on the east end of the marsh) and Griswold (located on the other end off to the west) regarded the eight-mile-long wetland as a basic pain. Snaking its way between the two communities, the area was a piece of acreage that was not tillable. In a wet year its fluctuating water levels could nearly always be

Even on a cloudy, rainy day, the bright iridescent green head distinguishes this mallard drake from other waterfowl species.

counted upon to flood adjacent croplands. Since there was no permanent means of crossing the area, people had to be content to drive around the marsh as opposed to scooting across the short distance from one side to the other. During dry periods, when passage was a possibility, the dense, mosquito-filled vegetation sprouting from the boggy area prevented locals from carving out little more than "turkey trail" crisscrossings which the following year were a good bet to be under water once again.

Even wildlife, especially ducks and geese, could not count on the marsh as a livable homestead. Rick Andrews and Lawrence Kelly hit the point hard when they joined me in my room around 3 o'clock that afternoon.

"Any year with big runoff would drown out all the emergent vegetation like the cattail and the bulrush," said Rick unfolding a topographical map out on a bed. "Once you've got that kind of lakelike situation there are no feeding zones for waterfowl, and it's almost as deadly as having too little water to play with. Let's face it, unlike a lot of God's creatures, ducks are awfully persnickety about where they make love. That's why we shoot for what we call a 'hemi-marsh' — a mix of half emergent vegetation and half open water.

"If you want successful waterfowl production you're going to have to have territorial sites for breeding pairs, nesting cover secure from predators, and high-protein food for egg-laying hens and growing ducklings," Rick explained. "You'll see the interspersion ratio of open water to vegetation out on Alexander Griswold, the kind of irregular pattern of edge which provides nesting territories with plenty of in-between space. Most ducks, you know, won't tolerate another pair of the same species within 100 feet of their territorial site."

Kelly, who was sitting in my chair by the air conditioner,

By adjusting Alexander Griswold's stoplog-control structures, water levels can be separately regulated in the project's six compartments.

Blue-winged teal forage on plants primarily, but one-quarter of their diet is animal life.

Greenwings, the smallest teal, are early migrators. Males leave the breeding grounds earlier than females, but females travel farther south than males.

had already eaten most of a bag of potato chips I'd bought earlier. He mumbled something about my ten years with DU— something to the effect that one would think I would have learned most of this by now. I told Kelly if he'd have explained it ten years ago as well as Rick was explaining it now we might already be out on the marsh instead of going through a briefing here in the room.

"What we're doing on Gris," continued Rick, "is to basically hold all the water we can. You've got to remember there

A wily coyote, always on the alert for mice and other small animals found on the prairies, directs its attention to a noise in the brush.

is no creek or river system, no permanent source of water for this marsh. It is very simply a varying contoured basin which fills or doesn't fill according to the availability of precipitation and snowmelt runoff. That snowmelt runoff is usually a slow melt in the spring and nowhere near so sensational as the torrential rush you'd see on those projects you visited out west."

"How did we get the green light to work on Griswold?" I asked. "Were the local people all for it or was it more complicated than that?"

Kelly seemed to perk up with this question. He has been with DU Canada for 34 years and has learned—if anyone has—how to get a proposed project off the drawing boards and into the light of day. At 55, he still has the quick wit and impish

humor which made him a special field companion years ago.

"Well what finally happened was this," said Kelly. "In 1976 we had one hell of a flood backing up out of the Alexander Marsh. At this point the local farmers had had it, so the municipalities, along with the help of the provincial government, attempted to drain the marsh into a creek that runs off to the west. But they were unsuccessful. They were going through nine feet of sand, and their ditch was fairly steep with a one-to-one slope that continuously silted in on them."

"So they quit?" I asked motioning to Kelly to throw me what little remained of my bag of chips.

"They quit the ditch business," Kelly replied, "and the municipality on the east end, which is Whitehead, got ahold of us to see if we could work something out. There was a bit of Crown land involved, really very little, because the majority of the land is in private ownership."

"You know that for a fact, don't you Lawrence," said Rick who laughed and slapped Kelly on the back.

"Yes I do," said Kelly who shook his head in a way that made it clear the time he was recalling was not an easy time. "When I did the negotiation to get the Alexander Griswold Marsh project approved there were 32 landowners involved. I know there were 32 because a lot of nights I counted them over in my sleep. You see, it took 32 agreements to get the project—31 of 32 wasn't good enough.

"What we were shooting for, of course, were 30-year lease agreements to control the water level of the marsh." Kelly stopped and looked at his watch, like maybe he was taking up too much time. I told him what he was saying was important to me, so he eased back in the chair and continued to talk. "You just don't go by a guy's place and go in there with him for 10 minutes and then propose a wetlands project. There are a lot of times I feel like a salesman with an empty

A twilight hunter, the crow-sized short-eared owl usually hovers quietly over the prairies and grass-lands searching for its prey. This individual seems to patiently await the cover of night.

A twilight hunter, the crow-sized short-eared owl usually hovers quietly over the prairies and grass-lands searching for its prey. This individual seems to patiently await the cover of night.

briefcase. You don't have cash to offer the guy or any-thing that he can really see. Just the whole concept of the project itself.

"It's not that farmers don't like wildlife. Most farmers do and want to see it around, but they want to know how much it's going to cost. So you may easily spend two hours with him, drink some coffee or a beer on his porch, and find out what his land problems really are, like the history of the marsh and its effect on his place. During this you might pick up on something he wants, like a small crossing or something he may have wanted for years but the price was just too much. Maybe he has had constant flooding problems so we'll try to figure how we might help correct that. Every landowner is different, and with the Alexander Marsh—or what came to be known as the Alexander Griswold Marsh project—we were fortunate in that there was really very little trade-off. This holds for most of the projects in our area, and there are 170 of them with some 460 landowners.

"I'll tell you what did my heart good," said Kelly. "When Alexander Griswold was dedicated to Illinois waterfowl biologist Frank Bellrose on July 2, 1983, it was one of the cooperating landowners who opened up his heavy-equipment shed when it started raining during the ceremony."

It was nearly five o'clock when the three of us drove out of Brandon in Rick's Dodge Ram toward the Alexander Gris-wold Marsh. The mugginess that had hung heavy in the ear-lier part of the day was being pushed out by a terrific-feeling high-pressure system that had dropped the temperature into the 70s. Gone was the haze and the harsh, glaring midday light, and in its place was a soft evening summer sun which cast sharp shadows across the forever-stretching bright greens of cereal crops.

Grain trains originating on the Canadian prairies often head east to Thunder Bay, Ontario, where the wheat, oats and barley are loaded on Great Lakes freighters for destinations overseas.

A grain train moves east. Rick says it is likely headed to Thunder Bay, and from there onto a Great Lakes freighter with a destination overseas. "They're just finishing up our first cut of hay," says Rick as he points to a farm rig rolling alfalfa into bales along the provincial right-of-way. "We only get two cuttings up here, four if you irrigate." He points to a field off to the left. "Fall rye," he says. "It should be ready for harvest within the next two weeks. The soil is light and sandy, and the rye grows three to four inches after it's planted

Stretching beyond this water-control structure is the kind of water/vegetation mix that helps provide Alexander Griswold's waterfowl quality nesting conditions despite the ravages of drought.

in the fall. That root system usually holds it through the winds of the big winter storms. Helps spread out the harvest season a little. A farmer can take this in early, then go on to barley, wheat or oats."

Rick is 30 years old. Originally from Winnipeg, he began project inspection work with Ducks Unlimited Canada right out of school with a zoology degree after attending the University of Manitoba. He has a relaxed feel about him, the kind of composure that is so much a part of people who like what they do. What he does is to evaluate potential sites for Ducks Unlimited marsh projects. He then follows through with engineers who design projects geared to stabilize marsh water

levels at depths which are known to be attractive to nesting waterfowl.

"The Alexander Griswold Marsh was designed with water management in mind," Rick says as we turn off pavement onto a gravel road by a bright blue field of flax. "Its acreage is divided into six independent cells or compartments with individual water-control structures. It's got 63 nesting islands, and is really one of the prettiest dabbler marshes that you are going to see in southwestern Manitoba. Before our program was initiated, you'd have runoff collect in the marsh basin early in the spring and spread out over the entire acreage. But because of the shallow depths that water would usually dry up by early summer. With our controls in place, we now have some portions of the marsh with adequate habitat even in drought years. And that is exactly what we've been having — the last five years have been the driest in the last 14."

We take another sharp turn, this one by a yellow field

"We had some tremendous sharp-tail shoots when I first moved to Brandon in 1977," said area biologist Rick Andrews. "The past two seasons, however, were disappointing not only to me, but to my Lab, Buckshot." Sharptails are not the only game bird found on the prairies. Upland hunters can also pursue grey (Hungarian) partridge and ruffed grouse.

which sweeps toward a patch of trees off to the north. "Rape," says Kelly, "or canola, it's the same thing. It's an oil seed, used for margarine and cooking oil." He reaches into a large grocery bag at his feet and comes up with a chunky looking ham and swiss cheese sandwich he had picked up at a quick-stop market on the edge of Brandon. Kelly gets to chewing on it, and the good, strong smell of mustard fills the cab of the truck.

"You see the bluff out there, eh?" asks Rick pointing off to my right. I look out toward the beginnings of a scrubby patch of woods which winds its way along the edge of a nice even-looking field of alfalfa. "We've had some tremendous sharptail shoots back in there," he says. "When I first moved to Brandon in 1977, from then on to 1981 is when they reached their cycle peak. It's been very poor the last two years. Buckshot is depressed."

Rick goes on to tell me he uses his eight-year-old Lab on waterfowl and upland game alike. In addition to sharptails there are ruffed grouse and grey partridge, which I think of as Hungarian. And when he's not chasing upland stuff or hunting waterfowl, he makes a point of hunting moose with Kelly.

"We don't fool with the trophy season," says Kelly. "We hunt the Red Deer Lake area, and stay in a 16-foot house trailer that I built. It's got plenty of insulation, and we set up a trapper's tent next to it with a wood stove where we store our gear and the Skidoos. Don't use the Skidoos to hunt, of course, just to get to an area and back again.

"Trophy season is usually the last week of September or first week in October with bulls only. The winter season is just for residents, usually tracking on snow back in the bush in December when you can take a cow or a bull. It's on the draw system, eh, and you seldom see anyone back in there during the day. It's plenty cold, and you get on a fresh track

45

DU COUNTRY

Though the out-of-focus creature behind these sunning mallard ducklings may look like the Loch Ness monster, it is actually the mother hen. In order to provide food and cover for her young, the hen leads her ducklings to water several hours after they hatch. She will stay close by until they learn to fly.

Although a coon will dine on nearly anything, the masked bandit, by nature, seeks its evening meal along the edge of a marsh. Today's intensive agricultural practices often make the search far too easy. Nest predation in many prairie wetland areas is extremely high.

and stay with it. You're on your own, really quiet. At noon you'll maybe stop and boil a pot of tea. I enjoy it."

"There's a brood of cans," says Rick happily. We are fifteen miles from Brandon, on the east end of the Alexander Griswold Marsh, about one mile from the project's main water control. I watch the seven tiny canvasback ducklings, and Rick points off to the left. "Another brood," he says. "Six mallards and their mama."

The project is one beautiful piece of water. A great blue heron stalks the dark green edge of some hard-stem bulrush. A killdeer moves behind a pair of American avocets on a mud flat, and Richardson's ground squirrels scurry behind us along the gravel road.

We climb back in the truck. Our next stop is Alexander Griswold's main control — two large culverts sunk in a flared concrete wall with a stoplog base. A large black-and-yellow garter snake chases minnows in a clear pool of water below us. "You can think of this as the final control for any water that comes through the project," says Rick. "It essentially regulates all the water from here to the west end, though we can of course individually regulate levels within each compartment by maneuvering the stoplogs."

As we move downhill to take a closer look at the structure, the garter snake spooks and I see how far down the water level on the control really is. "In a normal July, you would see the level of water down around 10 inches," says Rick. "Right now it is down three and a half feet from the top. Look, it's no longer even registering on that water gauge. What we

The blue shoulder patch on a resting blue-winged teal is covered with brown feathers. But when the bird takes flight, it is the bright blue feathers that distinguish it from other species.

This American avocet pair embraces gracefully in what may well be the beginning of courtship behavior. One way to distinguish male and female is by the upturned bill. In the female it is considerably more exaggerated.

don't have is what the engineers call a "head" of water, something to work with. In other words, a quantity we could push back to the west end."

I turn for a moment to watch Kelly who is kneeling by the water's edge pointing to a series of coon tracks, and Rick continues his thoughts. "When Mother Nature pulls the rug out from under you like she has for the last five years of this drought, you have to adjust. Because we want to hang onto at least some water at all costs through the brood season, which runs mid to late August, we decided to keep the stoplogs in

all of our controls so each compartment will catch runoff as best it can. As a rule, in previous years, we kept the logs out of the controls and let the water spread through the entire marsh. But after five drought years, we've not been able to hold water any longer in cells one and two on the west end. But the rest of them are holding their own, and the broods we're seeing here tonight will have the water they need to see them into flight."

As we climb the bank to the truck, we look back upstream as a brood of shovelers (Rick says they are three to four weeks old) floats around a stand of cattail in the early evening light. A near-full moon is slipping up from the eastern horizon, and the smell of fresh-cut hay is everywhere.

"I guess what I'm saying is that when you have very little water you can't manipulate water levels as you would like," says Rick. "On the other hand, though Alexander Griswold may be temporarily a little low, at least it is *there*."

Maritimes

From a sportsman's point of view, it's hard to beat the Maritimes. For the hunter, there's pheasant, waterfowl, ruffed grouse, woodcock, moose and white-tailed deer. And for the fisherman, Atlantic salmon, sea-run brook trout and striped bass.

He had decided to take the American to the Amherst Marsh. The marsh was only 15 minutes outside of town and they were running out of time. It was the second day of the Nova Scotia duck season and he knew the hunting pressure would have slacked off from yesterday. Whether they would have a crack at a black duck this evening, however, was something else again.

That, he gathered, was what the American really wanted. But because the local birds on the marsh had been worked over on the opener he knew they could not count on any blacks. There would be woodies working tonight to be sure. Along with them would likely be some teal, ringnecks and wigeon. The island, up on the east end, would be where a flock of late-incoming black ducks would head. The other birds would pitch in anywhere at dusk, but having hunted the island for nearly 20 years he went with what he felt was their best shot.

On their way down the east-side channel, he soon realized they traveled with some luck. He had not seen any freshly chewed up vegetation on the edges from outboard props. And by the time they passed the big shoreline stand of paper birch, where he swung the boat out into a narrow cattail-lined passage toward the marsh's center, he had not heard any shooting. Though he had seen only two small flights of birds, they would at least have the island to themselves.

He had shut off the motor and poled them into a thick stand of bulrush with the big island right behind them and the little spit of land out front. The big island was grown up in mature white spruce, while the little peninsula was covered with a thick stand of speckled alder. His old Chesapeake, whose name was Patty, lay quietly in the bottom of the boat while he had tossed out a dozen light plastic decoys. He put little effort into brushing the boat's sides with the bulrush. At this time of evening the birds would have already decided whether they wanted to roost off the edge of the big island or not.

49

The black duck is often considered the most wary of all waterfowl species. It tends to seek remote areas for nesting opportunities, but in maritime country, once a brood can fly, the family is quick to head to a nearby salt marsh.

Half an hour passed and off in the distance they watched the lights along the north side of Amherst come on. It was a clear night—going to be a cold one—and he was glad he'd brought a down coat for his friend. Not that it was too uncomfortable sitting in the blind; he and Patty and the American were crouched together below the bulrush. The time for the heavy coats would come with the boat ride back to the parking lot against the wind.

He had begun sipping his second cup of hot thermos coffee

when six big ducks dropped in low over the paper birch. They continued toward the spread, then swung wide and to the left behind the speckled alder. Patty whimpered, and his friend kept his face down and head low. At first he thought they had continued north across the marsh behind the spit of land. But suddenly there they were, all six of them blacks, coming out from behind the speckled alder and into the decoys.

"Easy, Yank," he whispered. "Easy. Now!"

"It's my home," said maritime manager Allan Glover. "I grew up in Nova Scotia, then did my share of knocking about living here and there like anyone else. We were out in Alberta, in Edmonton, but moved back to the Maritimes six years ago. To me there's no other place quite like it on earth.

"The winters are not really hard. You get a nice long fall starting at the end of August when you might have some frost, but freeze up doesn't come 'til the end of November, with snow not really sticking until Christmas. Now and again the summer gets hot and a little sticky, but you've got the sea breezes at night to cool things down. Like they say in the Maritimes, 'if you don't like the weather wait 10 minutes and it'll change.' That may be stretching it a bit, but it really does change dramatically overnight.

"From a sportsman's standpoint it's pretty tough to beat. The woodcock shooting is some of the finest you will find anywhere. There's ruffed grouse and pheasant, excellent waterfowl shooting, moose and white-tailed deer. So far as fishing goes, trout is pretty much king today, though Atlantic salmon certainly continues to be a big draw. We still have the giant bluefin tuna off Prince Edward Island, and in the rivers there are Atlantic salmon, sea-run brook trout and striped bass."

It is October 2, 1985, and I'm in Ducks Unlimited Canada's Amherst, Nova Scotia, regional office with Al, maritime

The woodcock, a unique upland shorebird, is found in alder thickets and woodlands where its mottled colors blend in with the dead leaves of the forest floor. A popular game bird, some of the finest woodcock shooting in the world can be found in the Maritimes.

The richness of wetlands is reflected in the variety of plant life found there year-round, from spring's blooming wildflowers to fall's frost-covered grasses.

The Maritimes support healthy populations of Eastern white-tailed deer. "For the first time since the late 1960s," says DU Canada area biologist John Wile, "Nova Scotia will permit resident hunters to take two deer this season of either sex."

biologist Keith McAloney and area biologist John Wile. The Maritimes—Newfoundland, Nova Scotia, New Brunswick and Prince Edward Island—are part of DU Canada's eastern region which also includes Ontario and Quebec. The fact that over half of the region's 571 wetland projects are located in the Maritimes interested me, but even more intriguing was the kind of conditions Glover and crew confront in their daily construction work.

"Think back about what you saw out west on the prairies," Al said. He is intense, enthusiastic about what he is explaining, and takes time out for a sip of coffee and a long drag on a cigarette. There is an alive and joyous quality in his eyes which suggests to me that he's made a point of savoring daily living. "Out there you have a spillway that's made to take a peak flood maybe once a year. Here there is water all around you, flowing all year long, so we design structures with that in mind. We've developed some 40,000 quality wetland acres in the Maritimes with 130 fishways involved in the program. In Edmonton you'll get maybe 18 inches of rain in a year. In the Maritimes we'll annually total, including runoff, probably 49 to 52 inches. So when you get out in the field this afternoon with John you'll see more concrete in our water-control structures than you have anywhere else. Concrete, and steel sheet piling."

Structural material, I soon found, is not the only factor which distinguishes the maritime wetlands program from its prairie or mountain counterparts. There are other very basic differences, and Keith—who has spent 13 years in the mari-

It is only natural, when you think of the common loon, to recall the loud yodels and melodic laughter that are so much a part of its repertoire of calls. Loons are found onshore only during breeding and nesting seasons. Here, a female swims with her young.

time program – explained them to me.

For starters, I learned it's important to realize that in DU Canada's coastal program the biologists and engineers are not dealing with the "whole" marsh. The French Acadians were the first to do that in the 1600s when they went about diking and ditching vast expanses of saltwater tidal marsh complexes along both the Bay of Fundy and the Northumberland Strait. This process was not new to them. They had fine-tuned the mechanics of it on France's Normandy coast before moving to the Maritimes and founding Port Royal in 1605. By

constructing an *aboiteau* – think of it as a swinging door or flap gate – at the bottom end of a marsh where the marsh meets the sea, the Acadians could shut off the flow of salt water during an incoming tide. Outgoing fresh water could also be controlled, and the ultimate result was the build up of silt at the mouth of the estuary which made for rich agricultural soil.

Then came the English, who distrusted the politics of the French enough to kick them out of the Maritimes in the 1750s. The English took stock of the marshland acreage their predecessors had reclaimed from the sea and decided that though the politics of the French was not to their liking, the nutrient-rich soil was attractive indeed. So the English continued the laborious digging and shifting of tidal earth until virtually all the salt marshes along the Bay of Fundy were diked.

After experimentation with this and with that, it became clear that hay was, hands down, the crop most likely to enhance the economy of a local area. The sale of it remained profitable through the 1920s. During this period hay barns were a common site along tidal estuaries throughout the Maritimes. But then came increased mechanization and the automobile. Soon, hay no longer had a viable market, and by the 1940s the hay barns were fast becoming a thing of the past. Agricultural operations were abandoned, and incoming tides once again began to take control of the land.

"That is the key to it," Keith said. "Our coastal wetlands program focuses on the 'top end' of these marshes, the part that slopes back from the built-up silted area down by the sea. We start out with this acreage that's little more than a hodgepodge of ponds, marsh and swamp. And what we come up with is a series of carefully controlled freshwater impoundments which really do make a difference when it comes

Thanks to this DU Canada water-control structure and fishway, the village of Hillsborough, New Brunswick, can observe and enjoy waterfowl on the local project and catch sea-run brook trout too.

In the fall, the marbled godwit, like many other shorebirds, leaves its nesting grounds for wintering areas. From July through August, hundreds of thousands of shorebirds drop by the intertidal flats of New Brunswick's Mary's Point where they beef up on marine amphipods (small crustaceans).

to the nesting success of the birds."

It is nearly eleven o'clock and Al gets us all some fresh coffee. Between running tape and scribbling notes, I've not said a lot, and John Wile wonders if I'm antsy. I tell him it's not so much that, as it is the information they've given me. Fascinating stuff, but different from the basic DU program material I'm familiar with – different enough that I'm pushing hard to keep up with what they're saying. And there is something else. Outside the windows of the office is one of the prettiest autumn days I've seen so far this year. There are no clouds, and at most it is a very slight breeze that flutters the leaves of a young maple. One thing I do not have to be told is that Nova Scotia's waterfowl season opened yesterday, October 1. I mention casually to Keith that it has been nearly 10 years since I've shot a black duck.

"If we slack off on that pot of coffee and get you out in the field with John for a look at some projects," says Keith, "you may get back here to meet me in time to change that tonight."

John Wile joined DU Canada's staff fresh out of college with an Acadia University biology degree in 1975. In a relaxed yet steady pace we tour maritime DU country snaking along the 17 miles of Nova Scotia/New Brunswick border between the head of the Bay of Fundy and the Northumberland Strait. There is bright afternoon sunshine and the salty smell of tidal flats and the sea. The farms are tiny by prairie standards, but John explains that visiting westerners come to respect their productivity. Apples flourish here, and the potato industry is big in New Brunswick and Prince Edward Island. Wild, low-bush blueberries are a maritime specialty, as is maple syrup gathered in the spring from the hardwood ridges. "A big farm here is 200 to 300 acres," says John. "Because it is very heavy land due to the build up of silt from the action of

the tide, there is a drainage problem. Farmers adjust to that with a technique known as 'hill and crowning.' See the lay of that land off to the right? The farmer has contoured his plowing upward so that the field is high in the center. See how the edges fold down for better drainage?"

John explains that DU Canada began "picking away" in the Maritimes in the early 1960s, but didn't really make a strong go of it until the Amherst, Nova Scotia, office was opened in 1971. The staff could cover southern New Brunswick out of the Amherst base, but in 1978 an office was opened in Fredericton and the rest of New Brunswick's DU wetland operations came to be efficiently coordinated out of there.

The size of the maritime projects varies from the huge 6,000-acre Missaquash Marsh to the tiny freshwater compartments of Hillsborough Marsh (48 acres) and the 27-acre, two-segment complex at Baie Verte. Though their acreage totals differ, the basic approach to water-control operations does not. Each, as Keith had explained earlier, depends on the

At low tide, in maritime country, a host of small fish, birds and other wildlife can be found on the vast expanse of flats. While raccoons, mink and herons concentrate on shallow pools filled with minnows and fairy shrimp, osprey and eagles search for meals while soaring in the sky above.

downstream existence of an *aboiteau* which keeps out the sea. In nearly all cases this flap gate has been constructed and is maintained by the provincial agricultural agencies. It is on the "top end" of the marsh, farther inland from the sea, that DU Canada concentrates its operations. Hillsborough Marsh, located in New Brunswick on the Bay of Fundy, was a case in point.

The *aboiteau* and dike located several miles downstream from the Hillsborough project was likely first put in place, John explained, in the 1600s. While the bottom end of the marsh supported haying operations, the top end proved too wet. Before DU Canada's construction program began in 1983 the area was little more than a large, thick stand of cattails with a stream which could barely wind its way down through the middle. Within a year after the installation of a main dike, a water-control structure and a five-pool fishway, the Hillsborough Marsh looked to me like a scene out of Currier and Ives.

The sparkling piece of water is surrounded by a wooded, upland edge of mainly conifers—black, white and red spruce with a bit of poplar. Beyond the conifers is a hardwood ridge of maple, and it is not difficult to imagine its coloration with the first frost. As John and I stand by the fish ladder and look upstream, sea-run brook trout are rolling on the surface along vegetation which cuts out toward open water.

"The village of Hillsborough is very happy with it," says John as we listen to the soft, trickling sound of clear, cold water. Last winter they used it for ice skating, and this spring they were plenty pleased with the quality of fishing they had on the trout."

We leave Hillsborough and continue our early afternoon drive along the west side of the Peticodiac River to where it empties into Shepody Bay. "This entire area was formerly salt

Many of DU Canada's smaller maritime coastal projects are surrounded by uplands and mixed hardwoods. Between the upland and water's edge there is often old-field vegetation offering waterfowl quality nesting areas.

marsh," says John, "diked up near the Bay of Fundy's edge. For hundreds of years they've farmed it for hay. See those beef cattle grazing out there? Nothing here has really changed." The day remains sunny, and we pass through several pretty southern New Brunswick towns which take me back to earlier years spent in New England. The leaves of the hardwoods are beginning to turn; it is cool, and there is the smell of wood smoke in the air.

Outside the small community of New Horton is DU Canada's 433-acre New Horton project constructed with funds donated by Maryland's Easton Waterfowl Festival. Pintails, blue-winged teal, ringnecks and black ducks are some of the species which look to the project's fresh water for nesting and staging opportunities. We are not far from Fundy National Park. To the north of us is a small project near Mary's Point, which John explains is considered to be one of the most important shorebird migration sites in North America.

"There are tremendous buildups of shorebirds which come through the Maritimes in the summer from the Arctic on their way to South American wintering grounds," says John. "Millions of them, mainly plovers and sandpipers. By mid-September they are gone, but come the last part of July and through August there are flocks of 100,000 to 200,000 birds gathered on the intertidal flats around Mary's Point. You'll find short-billed dowitchers, least sandpipers, red knots,

Some people might think of the white-winged scoter as little more than a fat sea duck. It is indeed the largest of the scoters, and in order to gain the momentum necessary for takeoff, it "runs" along the water's surface for quite a distance before it can lift its heavy body into flight. Sea duck hunting has recently become more popular, not only in the Maritimes, but all over the U.S.'s Northeast Coast.

dunlin and both semipalmated and black-bellied plovers. They feed mainly on a small amphipod, beefing up their fat reserves for the long, over-water flight south."

We make our way back up the Peticodiac, then swing north along the Nova Scotia/New Brunswick border to the Northumberland Strait. Out across the big tidal flats there is a strong wind blowing the spartina grass. It is beginning to yellow with autumn, and as far as I can see, duck blinds dot the potholes. "They're into mainly local birds," John says. "Serious hunting begins in November when we get the northern flocks. The fair-weather boys will have called it quits by

then. That's when you start to see the real duck hunters.

"The Northumberland Strait is much warmer than the Bay of Fundy. The beaches are sandier, not like the rugged cliff shoreline we saw back at New Horton. You find the summer crowd along here – people from Amherst and Moncton who have bought a second home. My family and I have fun just making a day of picnicking on the strait. All the others figure they've made it with a beach cottage," he grins. "I figure they've ended up with two yards to mow."

We come to the tiny town of Baie Verte on the New Brunswick/Nova Scotia border. "If you continue north along the coast," John says, "you'll begin to find more French-speaking people. The farther north you go the less likely you'll find people who speak English." There is a DU Canada project here in Baie Verte and we stop to take a look.

"This is part of a large salt-marsh complex," he explains. "We selected this top section to work on; it was only partly tidal. We cut off the tide with a dike and a tidal gate and came up with 27 acres of what amounts to freshwater impoundment. There are two segments here – two dikes and two water-control structures. The birds can't really nest in the salt marsh itself because of the tide fluctuations. But they do pair in it. That's where a project like Baie Verte comes into play. It offers stabilized levels of fresh water to nesting waterfowl. Once the brood is ready to fly, they'll make their way back to the salt marsh."

Like the Hillsborough project, Baie Verte is surrounded by upland with old-field vegetation. Goldenrod, which makes excellent nesting areas, sweeps up toward a mixed woodland of tamarack and spruce. Off in the distance I see the top of a white church steeple in the town. Beyond it, whitecaps are breaking with the wind on the Northumberland Strait.

"All of us still value our work on the big marsh complexes,

The changing colors of the hard-wood trees in the Maritimes rival even those found in New England.

The common merganser forages for fish by dipping its head, up to its eyes, underwater, or by diving. The serrated edges of its bill, which are responsible for its nickname—the sawbill—help it to catch and hold fish.

don't get me wrong," says John. We're walking through timothy grass along the edge of Baie Verte's upper segment. Cormorants, a pair of great black-backed gulls and several herring gulls explore the far edge of the project as we talk. "But we have wetland inventories that tell us what we've got out there for development and it's clear we're going to be working on smaller areas. To tell you the truth, if I had a choice between working on one 50-acre marsh or five 10-acre marshes, I'd go with the little ones. We'd come up with more duck production and more wildlife. Add to that the fact that more people would be exposed to the work of DU."

It is late afternoon and the sun is gone, slipped behind a cloudbank that has blown out of the northeast. Twice during our drive along the strait I've seen small flocks of waterfowl working offshore against the wind and I think back on Keith's morning offer of a black duck hunt. We are standing in a

The highly colorful feathers of the wood duck are prized by flytiers everywhere. Low populations of the bird earlier this century have increased tremendously through wood duck nesting box programs. The woodie is now the most abundant breeding duck in the eastern United States.

parking lot by a tidal flap gate which DU Canada cost-shared with the provincial department of highways on Wallace Bay. All around us there are cars and trucks whose owners are scattered over the 765 acres which make up DU Canada's Wallace Bay #4 project. They are getting sporadic shooting—the sound of five quick shots rumbles across the marsh.

This whole area was saltwater tidal inlet. Once it was diked hundreds of years ago, horse-drawn equipment harvested hay crops until increased mechanization made it impossible to continue farming over the rough terrain. By 1950, the marshland was nearly totally abandoned, save for some pasture. And in 1971, the Canadian Wildlife Service acquired the acreage, which was little more than a heavily vegetated composite of ponds, marsh and swamp.

DU Canada began water-control operations on 140 acres of Wallace Bay #1 in 1972 and 1973 through contributions from the Downeast Chapter of Maine. One hundred sixty more acres were added to the complex through dragline diking operations during the late summer of 1973 on Wallace Bay #2. With the completion of section #4, brood counts in the area began to rise dramatically. When work first began the acreage might at best have supported 10 waterfowl families. Today it routinely produces 80 broods. Green- and blue-winged teal frequent the area in addition to black ducks, northern pintail and shovelers, American wigeon, ring-necked ducks and hooded mergansers. In 1979 it proudly hosted the first brood of redheads recorded in the Maritimes.

"It is an excellent piece of brood and staging habitat," says John as we walk out a cattail-lined section of Wallace Bay dike. "The land here is not really as flat as it looks, so we built a series of dikes along the side of this major water impoundment we're looking at in order to control water levels within the different sections." A bittern suddenly flushes from thick vegetation beneath John's feet, and I'm pleased that John jumps. I have come to like him a lot, but there's some humor in watching the bittern shake his disciplined biologist's cool.

"Nothing is simple of course," he continues, still laughing about the bittern. Two more shots ring out several hundred yards off to our left. "In 1984 the *aboiteau* broke and a big fall tide washed over the top of our dikes. So in addition to rebuilding the *aboiteau,* we had to re-top our dikes. This time we designed the tidal gate in a way that it can easily be repaired. That was the trouble with the old one. In order to work on it we'd have to wait for one or two of the lowest tides of the year. With this one we can drop stoplogs into the front and back of it. Once they are in place we simply pump the water out of the middle section and go to work. That tide took out a bunch of our bulrush and cattail. But as you can see, this vegetation is coming back real nice."

It's grown colder, and during the drive back to the motel John turns the heater on. When we arrive I find Keith sitting in the lobby. He wears a beat up duck hunting hat that's pushed back high off his forehead. "You're probably too tired after all that traveling to push out of here for a black duck hunt aren't you, Yank?" I tell him I'll meet him outside in about the time it will take him to start the engine of his pickup.

"How many of us who live north of the Rio Grande know that within the borders of our neighbor republic to the south there is embraced a territory larger than that of France, Germany, Italy, Spain, the Netherlands, Belgium and Switzerland combined? That within her borders practically every product of the soil of the tropical and temperate zones can be grown to perfection?"

–Dillon Wallace
 Beyond the Mexican Sierras,
 1910

Mexico

"There isn't anything out there," says Singleton, "that in one way or another won't bite, sting or stick you." Cruising along in the Wagoneer, I believe him. Way off against the horizon across the mesquite it is not difficult to imagine Clint East-wood materializing out of a dust devil, head down and riding hard having been beat up by a bunch of guys you can bet were no good. Because the soil is limestone, moisture absorption is slow and fast runoff routine. Prickly pear and jumping cactus are everywhere, as is catsclaw, bright yellow wild poppies and purple thistle. We pass through the small town of Pesqueria, Nuevo Leon. The midafternoon sun is uncomfortably hot, and the town's only street is quiet, without people. Breaking into open country once again there is a large crucifix by a sharp turn in the road. "Always the people place a cross by one who has been killed along the highway," says Emilio. "It is custom through all of Mexico."

"Is that ebony?" asks Matt. He is looking across the grays and the greens of sage to a patch of dark scrubby trees off in the distance. "It is," says Robert. "The heartwood is black, and the sapwood is yellow. Up in the Rio Grande valley of Texas it's the most important nesting habitat there is for whitewings and mourning doves. It's a dwarfy, dicotyledonous tree."

We turn, finally, off of the highway into country that calls out for four-wheel drive. After bouncing along the twisting, dusty road for maybe 10 minutes we scratch and haul our way to the top of a hill and suddenly, there it is: the Montfort project in the soft, diffuse light of a warm and windy spring afternoon.

It was on April 17, 1983 that Robert Singleton (currently DUMAC director of research) and Matthew Connolly (then DU director of development) and I flew to Monterrey, Mexico,

The roseate spoonbill builds its stick nest in bushes and low trees along Mexico's coastline. Here, the bird feeds its young. To catch prey, the spoonbill moves its spatulalike bill from side to side and snaps it shut around small fish or shrimp.

to begin a week-long inspection of Ducks Unlimited de Mexico (DUMAC) projects. It was a field tour which would push us through jungle and desert habitat alike – a trip which would be made in the good company of Emilio Rangel-Woodyard (DUMAC's director of conservation) and Federico Kleen (director of construction engineering).

To comprehend the need for DUMAC, you must first realize that "conservation" (as you likely know it) simply does not exist to your everyday Mexican. Poverty is something he understands, but the concept of conserving a precious natural resource for posterity is, with good reason, unknown to him. He will conserve it for the amount of time that stretches between when he takes a duck in the morning and when he shares it with his family at night, but given the hard-nosed parameters of his survival, he is not interested in conserving a natural resource for much longer than that.

It was in the late 1960s and early 1970s that Ducks Unlimited began to explore channels through which a conservation

The white-winged dove continues to draw large numbers of U.S. hunters to Mexico for fast, early September wingshooting. While regulations used to be nearly nonexistent, the Mexican Fauna Silvestre (federal department of wildlife) now keeps strict tabs on bag limits.

ethic, however rudimentary, might be introduced to Mexico. What was needed was a financial anchor inside Mexico, a source from which a conservation momentum could be established. Robert Singleton was soon to become instrumental in locating this source.

In 1972, Singleton was referred to Alejandro Garza Lagüera. Years ago the Garzas, along with four other families, formed a private enterprise industrial complex which is today one of Mexico's largest conglomerates – Monterrey's Alfa and Visa groups. The five original founding families eventually

The flamingo differs from the spoonbill in several ways. The most apparent are the bill, which is thick, black-tipped and bent down from its small, round head, and the neck, which is longer than the spoonbill's.

61

Looking out from the conifers in its low-mountain habitat in Mexico, the golden eyes and black spots distinguish this jaguar from other cats, like the ocelot or mountain lion.

These DUMAC-constructed nesting islands on the Montfort project are ready for grassy-edge plantings of bulrush and smartweed. The teal, gadwall, baldpate, shovelers and pintail attracted to the project's 165 acres begin arriving in October.

sifted down to two. The Sadas generated the machinery which produced Alfa group; the Garzas sparked Visa group which today boasts over 50,000 employees.

As director general of the Visa brewery, Alejandro Garza provided the force needed to launch Ducks Unlimited's hopes for the creation of a Mexican conservation ethic. At first the effort and accompanying investment was small. In 1974, the breweries put up about $30,000 to take some of Ducks Unlimited's films and translate them into Spanish. Slowly, a staff was assembled, and top Visa executives such as Dr. Eric W.

Gustafson were placed in DUMAC administrative volunteer slots to ensure the fulfillment of the conservation dream.

"Take the Lerma project," said Eric, who is now DUMAC's executive vice president. "Look back and you will see there is a great deal we have learned. A secretary graciously brings coffee on a tray. We are in Eric's office following a tour of DUMAC's Monterrey headquarters. "Lerma was chosen because of its high visibility, so close to Mexico City."

I had heard about the Lerma project. It was DUMAC's first significant attempt at wetlands restoration, a vast undertaking that is not complete to this day. This is not to say that it will not be completed, only to point out that it was here where everyone involved learned how complicated the launching of an environmental ideology can be. For starters, all of Mexico's surface water is owned by the government. To construct water-control structures, particularly on the acreage encompassing Lerma, is to set the stage for an alley fight that could drag on for years and years.

There is, first off, an agreement with water resources officials. There is the permit from the department of agriculture (this because Lerma involves *ejido* land – land which is for all practical purposes owned by the government, but loaned to farmers on a co-op basis as long as the individual makes efforts to keep the acreage productive). The department of commerce is interested because fisheries may in one way or another be affected. And finally, the department of health wants a piece of the action, as do tourism agencies which require an agreement with the state's governor.

"In no way am I saying Lerma was poor business," says Eric. At 38 years old he radiates an energy that translates quickly and easily into a successful pattern of disciplined daily business. "What I am pointing out is that I feel we have come a long way from Lerma in that we have learned so very

DUMAC first moved its water-control operations into desert country with the Tulillo project located 35 miles northwest of Saltillo. Here, a black-tailed jackrabbit washes up on the desert where bathwater comes at a premium.

A truly global duck, the fulvous whistling duck breeds in all four hemispheres. It has been found throughout the United States, Canada, Mexico, South America, Africa and Asia, from the lowlands to several thousand feet above sea level.

much. Many of the projects you'll be looking at—two of them this afternoon—are examples of that knowledge. Sure, we still become involved in project sites on government lands, but whenever possible I like to see us deal with privately owned acreage."

He shakes his head and on comes an engaging Gustafson smile. "Lerma does feature visibility, but so does the Montfort complex that you are about to see. I was really tickled to discover that many commercial Mexican flights coming into Monterrey are now dipping the wings of their aircraft to let the passengers take a peek at the projects below. The visibility is essential, for people must see and talk about our projects if they are to learn what conservation really means. On the other hand, you must remember that there are sometimes security dues which come with all this, for the poverty factor is always there. At Lerma, for instance, we constructed a huge billboard explaining what our management program was all about. Within two months it had been cut down by the local people for firewood."

We all get out of the Wagoneer and scramble to higher ground. Way off to the west, the peaks of the Sierra Madre Oriental are etched light purple in the late afternoon sun. Below us some bluewings and a little bunch of shovelers make their way in and around the Montfort project's nesting islands. There is absolutely no sound up here on the hill save the strong wind blowing across the mesquite.

A harmonious whistlelike call accounts for the black-bellied whistling duck's name. The red-billed duck prefers mudflats and sandbars such as those found in the tropical coastal areas of Mexico.

A part of the project's impact might be lost if you did not bear in mind that aside from the water which is being held here and on neighboring Penitas, there is very little moisture of any consequence for miles around. There is, of course, the Ayancual River, but it is the river itself that has contributed to environmental problems in this dry country, 40 kilometers northeast of Monterrey. Monterrey's industrial growth did not come about without cost. The Ayancual, a medium-sized stream whose flow force has everything to do with the cycles of the rainy season, is filled with the oils and other wastes that make Monterrey the industrial heavyweight that it is.

When he was a boy, Alejandro Garza hunted these marshes along the Ayancual. So you see, in this instance, the wetland restoration work being done here has much to do with dreams—the dream of a man who is at a point in his life that he'd like to think about something special being passed on for hunting generations to come.

The Montfort legacy is this. As DUMAC restoration work continues, five marshes along the Ayancual that long ago ran out of quality habitat will once again offer attractive feeding, nesting and cover features to many species of waterfowl. Over the years, Alejandro's beloved childhood marshes had deteriorated in water-carrying capacity thanks to siltation from adjacent croplands and slow-but-sure loss of a dependable water supply. At Montfort, an inlet from the river has been constructed, one that will admit water from the base—not the surface—of the polluted Ayancual. A wire structure designed to hold hay bales has been installed in order to filter surface industrial oils.

The islands have been planted with grassy edge from local supplies of bulrush, spikerush, pond weed, smartweed and duckweed. Nesting boxes have been installed for the native muscovy duck and black-bellied whistler, but Montfort's 165 acres will attract "mostly your puddlers" according to Emilio. Teal, gadwall, baldpates, shovelers and pintails begin arriving in October, then spend the winter in and around the protective, nutritious edges of Montfort's island complex. When they pull out in early spring for nesting habitat far to the north, the birds have physically rebounded from the wear and tear incurred during the long, exhaustive fall flight of the previous year. Throughout his descriptions there is a pride in Emilio's tone; a comparable excitement, a look of having succeeded, can be seen in Federico's eyes.

This green heron seems pleased to have healthy mangroves available while it seeks shelter from the mid-day heat. At times the bird will actually dive completely under-water in an effort to secure its prey.

DUMAC's wetland efforts have helped restore populations of Mexico's wild muscovy duck. The muscovy is a strong flier, with drakes weighing up to nine pounds. The bird is now protected in all of Mexico's 29 states.

We walk, here and there kind of slide, back down the hill to the car. The Penitas marsh, says Emilio, is just a hop, skip and jump around the corner.

Two chachalaca explode from the pluchia (a broomweed) along the river. Brown jays holler from the underbrush. A blue-rock pigeon comes highballing overhead. We park the Wagoneer under a grove of ebony, walk around a bend, and there is the treat of island construction going on here at Penitas. It is quite a sight.

The locally hired contractors have set up camp on the edge of the construction site. At the moment, they are filling the big caterpillars with diesel fuel. Sausage hangs from the trees by the tent. It is nearly seven o'clock, and in the fading light the long shadows have a richness that is autumnlike. Soon the sound of roosting boat-tailed grackles is everywhere. I want to get a different view of the islands, so I walk away from the construction, along the edge of the project, and come across a

The plumage of a pintail has all the deep-texture feel and subtle coloring of a fine English suit. The green speculum of the drake helps distinguish him in flight from the female whose wing patch is brown with a white trailing edge.

prickly pear cactus that sinks deep through my khaki field pants.

The islands – there are 26 on Penitas – are huge, each one easily two stories high. Unlike Montfort, which was filled from the Ayancual, Penitas will eventually fill with rainwater. For many seasons it has not been able to do so, not since the

A bird of the treetops, the chachalaca flies or hops from branch to branch, tree to tree, with one flock's cha-cha-lac *call causing another flock to respond.*

construction of a diversion channel years ago. When full, it will be comparable in size to Montfort. Its island edges will be planted with identical kinds of cover plants.

I walk over by an open mesquite fire to the Mexicans' campsite. The camp has a relaxed, content feel. The main man pets his dog, a boxer, whose name just happens to be Dumac. Dumac looks like a sweet enough dog, but I don't think I'd try grabbing a sausage off of a tree limb.

When the entire Montfort complex is complete, there will be three more marshes to add to the Montfort and Penitas restoration list. Las Bravas, Presa Larga and Salsipuedes are future targets along the Ayancual. But for now, one step at a time.

By the time we hit the highway back to Monterrey, the day is pushing into sunset and we are all pretty much pooped. Matt spots three ibis way out in front of us, and *pauraques* (whippoorwill-like birds) flit against the deep yellows and reds of the evening sky.

VALUE OF A MARSH

When Ducks Unlimited Senior Writers George Stanley and Mike Beno first set off on these story assignments, I had no inkling then that their articles would eventually gel together the way they in fact do. Their trips held little in common from the standpoint of geography. Airline tickets involved destinations from as far north as The Pas, Manitoba, to the National Space Technology Laboratories in southwestern Mississippi; from the intensely cultivated prairie of western Minnesota to Utah's Bear River Marshes. Once the pieces were completed, however, several common thematic denominators emerged.

Wetlands are clearly under the gun every bit as much today as they were in what was to become known as the environmental 1970s, when our country first seriously began to respond to a national conservation conscience. And while Stanley and Beno are well aware that wetland drainage loss in the United States presently totals 460,000 acres a year, they chose, in their respective articles, to dwell less on this loss and more on the fascinating reasons why we should all make a point of preserving cattail country.

After reading the interviews featured in "Value of a Marsh" you will come to learn why some scientists now contend that wetlands may well be the most valuable type of habitat available on earth. Though you know that many farmers continue to ditch and drain their back-forty marshes, you will find that there are those who have managed financial success and actually improved the health of their land. You will meet fur trapper Big John Carriere of Cumberland House, Saskatchewan, and discover what wetlands mean to a people who for generations have depended on them for survival. And you will share the poignant reminiscing of a Utah waterfowler who finds himself without a marsh to hunt in the autumn of his years. —RW

A Scientist's Dream

By George Stanley

They're being used to purify sewage in cities and towns from San Diego, California, to Humboldt, Saskatchewan, and they could play a crucial role in solving future water shortage problems. They produce enormous quantities of plant and animal life that can be harvested for food, fuel, medicine and clothing, and they might one day even support human life in space.

Without them, mud laced with chemicals and fertilizers rolls unheeded and unfiltered off of farmland and into rivers and lakes. Without them, groundwater supplies dwindle, salts leach to the surface of the soil and cropland loses fertility. Without them, most of the commercially important fish species would cease to exist, as would our wild ducks and geese.

We're talking, of course, about wetlands – those soggy places that are too wet to call land and too lush to call water, places that our industrious society has been wasting out of ignorance even as scientists have begun to recognize them as perhaps the richest and most beneficial environments known to man.

"Wetlands can be managed for pollution control, for wildlife, for public recreation, for biomass production and for any number of other things," says Dr. B.C. Wolverton, senior research scientist for the National Aeronautics and Space Administration (NASA). The U.S. government recently honored Wolverton as its "Environmental Engineer of the Year." His enthusiasm for the benefits that wetlands have to offer is shared by G. Lakshman, a senior scientist for the Saskatchewan Research Council, who has spent the past 12 years developing practical ways to put wetlands to work.

Waste Treatment

Both Wolverton and Lakshman learned early in their wet-lands research that scientifically managed marshes can remove water pollutants more efficiently and less expensively than can conventional sewage treatment plants.

Lakshman set out in the late 1970s to develop "a viable sewage system which was economical for small towns." Small towns, he explains, generally can't afford conventional sewage treatment facilities. In an experiment supported financially by Ducks Unlimited, Lakshman created a series of artificial lagoons to clean wastewater from Humboldt, Saskatchewan, population 5,500. The cattails and reeds in Lakshman's marshes managed to successfully purify a substantial portion of the town's annual waste output during the plants' six-month growing season.

"Most plants take only enough nitrogen and phosphorous for themselves," Lakshman says. "Bulrushes and cattails take much more than they require." Nitrogen and phosphorous are nutrients found in human and animal waste. Primary ingredients of fertilizer, they are vital to plant life in measured doses. When too much nitrogen or phosphorous gets in your water, however, it becomes unsafe to drink. Beyond that, when high levels of these fertilizers enter rivers and lakes they prompt tremendous growth of weeds and algae. As the plants die and decay, the process of decomposition vacuums oxygen out of the water, killing fish – particularly game fish – which need more oxygen than bullhead, carp and other rough species. Sediment piles up; the bottom turns to muck; the water grows murky.

A main aim of sewage treatment is to remove excess nitrogen and phosphorous from wastewater before it is flushed into rivers and lakes. Lakshman's lagoons did more than that. Antibiotics released by the marsh plant roots destroyed potentially harmful bacteria found in human and animal feces. Marsh plants and organisms are also known to take in

Whitetail

dangerous chemical pollutants, such as PCBs, and break them down into harmless elements.

Wolverton first observed the cleansing power of wetlands in a Florida marsh. It was the late 1960s and he was developing defenses against biochemical warfare for the military. "I saw toxic chemicals disappearing into wetlands without a trace and with no apparent harm to the ecosystem," he says.

When the Defense Department scrapped its biowarfare research in the midst of Vietnam protests, Wolverton joined NASA and earned a PhD in environmental engineering to add to his previous training in chemistry and microbiology. At the National Space Technology Laboratories (NSTL) in southwestern Mississippi, Wolverton wears two hats as both a senior research biologist and the person who makes sure that the NSTL sewage discharges meet federal water-quality standards.

"In the mid-seventies our sewage-treatment plant wasn't meeting requirements," he says. "We were using outdated oxidation plants and mechanical package plants that were very expensive to maintain and operate. I said to our director at NSTL, 'Rather than spend millions on a new mechanical plant, why don't we just grow some wetland plants?' The engineering group laughed at the idea." Wolverton pauses for effect, leaning back and peering over his glasses. "Over the past 10 years," he says, "we've saved millions of dollars by cleaning the waste from this entire NASA site with *weeds*."

NSTL employs more than 4,000 people on a 150,000-acre site. All the waste in the place is treated by eight man-made wetland systems, the largest of them a seven-acre pond servicing the main building. Seven of the wetlands purify human sewage. The eighth removes heavy metals and other poisonous chemicals from the waste of several NSTL laboratories.

Deer commonly browse at the edge of the woods that surround the eighth facility while egrets wade in the water. The lagoon is 20 feet across, 2½ feet deep and it zigzags like a snake through a clearing in the southern pine forest. Wastes enter at the snake's head. Because the polluted water contains overloads of nutrients, plants grow thicker near the head of the snake than at its tail, where clear water trickles down a gravel-bedded creek.

"Our only upkeep on these systems is to harvest some of the plants once or twice a year," Wolverton says. "The systems are much less expensive to build and to operate than conventional wastewater treatment facilities. Even a small contracting company could take the research we've done and build wetland treatment systems that work as well or better than traditional facilities for a fraction of the cost."

Because they are so much less expensive to build and operate and because they are as flexible as nature itself, wetland sewage systems can be adapted to meet problems too little or too big for conventional facilities.

Cattail

Wolverton, for example, has designed a simple system that purifies discharge from his own septic tank which would otherwise leach into the soil, percolate down to the groundwater and seep into his backyard pond. Stones are buried in a shallow ditch lined with plastic, and wetland plants are rooted in the stones. Partially treated sewage from the septic tank flows through the stone filter, providing moisture and nutrients to the plants. When the water leaves this underground "wetland" it is pure enough to drink. Similar systems, Wolverton says, could be installed virtually anyplace where a body of water is dying before its time due to over-abundant weed and algae growth caused by excess nutrients from surrounding septic fields. The price landowners would have to pay to install such systems would be relatively small, he says, especially when you consider that waterfront land values depend greatly on the quality of the lake.

The more Wolverton learns about natural pollution control, the more potential he sees in it. He predicts that the low cost and high efficiency of these systems will enable wetlands to clean up messes that conventional treatment plants couldn't possibly handle. Wolverton has helped design an experimental water hyacinth system for San Diego that will soon be purifying a million gallons of wastewater a day. "Ninety percent of San Diego's water is imported – half from the Colorado River and half from northern California," he says. "The growth in Arizona is causing a greater demand for Colorado River water, and the farmers in northern California are continually fighting the cities in southern California for more water. San Diego is searching for alternative supplies for the future. They've looked into desalinization of ocean water but it's cost prohibitive. They came to us and asked if wetland systems could convert wastewater back into drinking water. We said, 'Sure,' and sent the engineering community into

convulsions. The city put together a panel of five consultants, and we designed an experimental system that purifies 25,000 gallons a day. It worked so successfully that the panel came up with a new system that will handle a million gallons a day. San Diego uses about 350 million gallons of water a day. I'd like to see them continue upgrading this pond system until it's eventually purifying half or more of that water up to potable standards."

A Little Action on the Side
Wetlands are not only cheaper than mechanical sewage-treatment systems, they also yield valuable by-products while eliminating waste.

In his Saskatchewan research, Lakshman has found that cattails and bulrushes make good, high-protein food for cattle, sheep and other livestock.

Cattails could become a common ingredient in human diets, Lakshman says, since their seeds yield a polyunsaturated oil of nearly identical quality to that of sunflower seeds. In fact, a recent study estimated that a hectare of cattails could produce 800 liters of oil compared to about 500 liters of oil per hectare of sunflowers.

Ecologist Eugene Odum determined that an acre of cattails can provide 5,500 pounds of edible flour with a nutritive value equal to or higher than that of rice, wheat or corn.

Japanese scientists have extracted a hormone from cattail pollen and are measuring its potential for stimulating improved growth of celery, tomatoes and other crops.

Cattail pollen may offer medicinal values as well. Chinese researchers have developed an anticoagulant drug from the pollen that inhibits plaque growth in arteries.

America's own National Institute of Cancer has taken *Juncus roemerianus*, a common marsh grass, and developed

Sampling water for impurities

Juncosol, an experimental drug that may prove useful in fighting some forms of leukemia.

"They're using *Juncus* in Egypt to desalinize cropland," Lakshman says. "They grow a crop of rushes and harvest it for three consecutive years, then plant a food crop. The rushes remove a lot of salt from the soil. We might be able to use this system in North America, where soil salinity is a rapidly growing problem."

Lakshman and others have proven that ethanol fuel can be economically distilled from many wetland plants. "Under the right conditions in a managed marsh," Lakshman says, "cattail rhizomes contain tremendous amounts of starch and sugars that can be used to make ethanol. An acre of cattails can produce the same amount of alcohol as an acre of corn. When you add in the cost of growing the corn—the cultivating and planting, the herbicides and fertilizers—cattails come out to be a much more economical source of ethanol."

Ethanol is only one of many forms of fuel produced by marshes, which Odum calls "the single richest ecosystem yet defined in terms of available energy." Lakshman is conducting a new experiment in which wood-burning furnaces fueled by cattails are heating homes in prairie Canada. "You wouldn't believe the heat these plants produce," he says. "Even with our harsh winters they're doing an excellent job of heating homes."

All power used to run the San Diego facility that Wolverton and his colleagues designed will come from methane gas produced from the wetland's water hyacinths.

In addition, the residue that remains after wetland plants are used to produce methane or ethanol makes excellent fertilizer, according to Wolverton. In fact, water hyacinths harvested from the NSTL lagoons are routinely used for fertilizer – except those taken from the snakelike system that handles toxic chemical wastes. "The water hyacinths in that particular lagoon absorb heavy metals like a sponge," he explains. "We bury them in a clay-lined pit where they decompose and concentrate. I call the pit our mine, because years from now there should be an economical way to reprocess those buried metals."

Many believe that economic gain from wetlands is an idea whose time has come. One man with this foresight is Herman Taylor, Jr., a past president and chairman of the board of Ducks Unlimited. More than 20 years ago, Taylor began examining the potential profitability of wetlands management. In the early seventies, he established the 11,000-acre Little Pecan Wildlife Management Area in southwestern Louisiana. There, a team of biologists scientifically manages Little Pecan's marshes and low-lying ridges to maintain optimum conditions for sustainably high yields of waterfowl, furbearers and alligators. The program also addresses the needs of game fish, timber, shrimp and crawfish. In addition, exploration for oil and natural gas is carried out without damaging Little

Pecan's productivity or scenic beauty.

Little Pecan is only one of many thousand large and astonishingly productive wetlands in North America. Odum determined that tidal marshes in Georgia produce 10 tons of organic material per acre each year—that rivals our most intensively farmed croplands. Of the 10 most commercially important fish and shellfish species, shrimp, salmon, oysters, menhaden, crabs, flounder and clams all depend for their survival on estuaries and associated wetlands—only lobsters, tuna and haddock do not. Much of our valuable timber grows in marshes, including white cedar, bald cypress and tupelo. So do cranberries and wild rice. Marsh hay can be used for grazing and mulch while other marsh grasses provide materials for baskets and cane chairs.

All of this continent's wild ducks and geese depend on wetlands; roughly 70 percent of them are hatched on marshes in the prairie states and provinces alone. Hundreds of bird species benefit from DU's wetland conservation projects in Canada, including eagles, hawks, owls, cranes, herons, loons, pelicans, pheasant, grouse, woodcock and a potpourri of migrating songbirds. DU's Canadian marshes help support several dozen mammal species as well, including elk, moose, deer, bear and wolves.

Wetlands in the United States are believed to support 5,000 species of plants, 190 species of amphibians and a third of all native bird species. As DU expands its habitat work into all 50 states, most if not all of these species are expected to benefit.

Ducks Unlimited wetlands—much like the marshes of Little Pecan Wildlife Management Area—are not merely saved from destruction, they are scientifically enhanced to be more productive than they could be if left in their natural state. This is especially important when you consider that by the mid-1980s the United States had lost an estimated 54 percent of the 215 million wetland acres believed to exist in 1776 and that we continue to lose a half-million acres of marshland per year in this country. Far fewer wetlands will mean far less wildlife unless those marshes that remain are made increasingly productive through management techniques, such as "drawdowns," in which biologists manipulate water levels to encourage an optimum mixture of food plants, cover vegetation and water.

Etcetera

Scientists are discovering that wetlands offer many other benefits to society besides their usefulness as wastewater-treatment facilities and biological factories.

There is, for example, their long-overlooked role in preventing floods.

According to nature's plumbing system, every year when

Alligator

the snows melt and the rains fall, water trickles to the lowland and settles in pools, from which spring oases full of life. But what happens when farmers and developers tinker with the plumbing in order to dry up the lowland so they can grow or build things on it? Now the water flows through ditches and drain tiles off one piece of land and onto another. The neighbor's marshes brim over, flooding land that had been dry; his tinkering moves the water farther still. Eventually the water, loaded with silt and fertilizers and pesticides and herbicides, reaches a stream and then a river. Other creeks bloated with water from drained lands empty in as well. The polluted river rises over its banks onto downstream farms, into downstream towns. One Minnesota farmer recently pondered the nearby Red River, considered by many to be an open sewer, which flows onward to North Dakota where for years it has been raising havoc with Fargo area farms. "It wouldn't surprise me," the farmer said, "to see the people around here get hit with a lawsuit from the fellas in Fargo for sending them the water that's been flooding out their fields."

Flood damages don't only affect the farmers involved, they hit all taxpayers since the federal government bails out badly flooded areas with disaster aid. The government also spends a great deal of money on flood-control projects that wouldn't be necessary if wetlands were kept intact.

In at least one instance the government has had the foresight to dam a flood at its source. Congress assigned the Army Corps of Engineers to create a flood-control plan for the Charles River Valley in eastern Massachusetts as it was being rapidly developed for housing and commerce. The Corps noticed that while floods caused severe damage on the lower Charles, where the river ran through Boston and Cambridge, there were few problems elsewhere along its 80-mile-long route. Areas around the upper and middle Charles escaped

flooding, the Corps discovered, thanks to 20,000 undeveloped acres of wetland within the river's watershed. During times of high water, the wetland basins absorbed the excess. In contrast, nearly all of the marshland that once existed in the Boston area had been drained. Even a flood-control dam there couldn't keep the waters from spilling over from time to time into basements, streets and subway tunnels.

The Corps of Engineers finally concluded that the government should purchase 8,500 critical acres of wetland in the river basin for water storage. "Nature has already provided the least-cost solution to future flooding," the engineers reported. "In the opinion of the study team, construction of any of the most likely alternatives – a 55,000 acre-foot reservoir or extensive walls and dikes – can add nothing." The Corps calculated that the government would prevent annual flood losses of roughly $1.2 million by conserving those 8,500 wetland acres.

Can anyone calculate what the annual destruction of *450,000* wetland acres is costing us in flood damages? What about the price of cleaning up the pollution that results when water is rushed across dirty fields to streams, rivers and lakes? Or of living with the filth because we can't afford to clean it up?

And I brought you into a plentiful country, to eat the fruit thereof and the goodness thereof; but when ye entered, ye defiled my land and made mine heritage an abomination.
The Book of the Prophet Jeremiah, 2:7

The Intangibles
So far, we have been dealing with scientific values of wet-

73

lands and science considers only those elements which can be fathomed with instruments, measured and documented. Scientists are fond of numbers, like the estimate one team of researchers made that society would have to pay between $50,000 and $80,000 to replace the functions that just one wetland acre performs. Equally fond of numbers are the "social scientists" – particularly economists. They can tell you that American hunters in the mid-eighties are spending about $300 million a year on licenses, permits, tags and stamps to pursue game birds and animals, many of which depend upon wetlands for their survival. They can also tell you that hunters have contributed more than $1 billion for wildlife management through the Pittmann-Robertson Act, which is funded by excise taxes on guns, ammunition and archery equipment. They can tell you that hunters, fishermen and outdoor enthusiasts spend more than $40 billion a year on guns and fishing rods and cameras and binoculars and film and boats and trailers and campers and trucks and motel rooms and so on and so forth. It's good that we have those numbers. As Lakshman says, "A lot of people won't listen to you unless you talk in dollars and cents."

But trite as it sounds, the people who are spending so much money for some time outdoors know that the most valuable things that wetlands offer cannot be described in dollars, cents or any other language.

It's not possible for us to gauge the impact of even one outdoor experience on an individual. It's not possible to know what is happening in a hunter
as he rows on dappled waters
that reflect the moon's pale light,
a breeze caressing his face
and rustling the reeds,
the oars dipping.

Songs of frogs and crickets and morning birds,
an orange line at the horizon, the sun
cracks open the starlit dome
and peeks inside; a gull
lifts off a post and twists its head,
deciding where to go.
A whee-whee-whistle of circling wings,
and thump of heart against chest,
a silence that seems absolute,
an absence?
No, the wings are set and slicing now,
tearing sky like fabric,
the hunter rises, swings,
a shot, an echo,
a bird falling,
falling, falling,
smacking water.
Ancient exhilaration,
then remorse . . .
Life fills up the hunter
on the marsh in the morning
while others lie in bed
asleep.

The Future
Forester Aldo Leopold created the discipline of wildlife management and wrote a collection of naturalistic essays titled *A Sand County Almanac*, which can be found on every outdoor writer's bookshelf. Leopold coined the term "land ethic" to describe a new way of dealing with the natural world, a way he predicted would prove necessary for the sustenance of life on earth, a way that requires man to view himself not as conqueror of the land but as citizen of it. "We shall hardly relin-

quish the steam shovel, which after all has many good points," he said, "but we are in need of gentler and more objective criteria for its successful use."

Leopold died in 1948. It would please him to see how the machines that have been used to destroy wetland habitats are now being used to save, enhance and even create them. Take for instance the bulldozer, which for decades farmers have used to wipe out trees and natural grasslands and fill in wetlands. DU is using bulldozers to build dikes and levees that collect runoff waters and form marshes.

Or take the backhoe, which for years landowners have used to dig drainage ditches. DU is using backhoes to dig channels that enable biologists to move water from one area of

Landsat

a marsh network to another, maintaining prime habitat conditions throughout the complex.

Take, even, the plow and cultivator, which DU is using to churn up sod and increase the fertility of bog wetlands. Or the tractor and planter, which DU is using to sow wildlife food and cover plants and to promote conservation farming practices, such as zero-tillage, that can benefit the farmer, the wildlife and the land.

Modern technology, often viewed as an unnatural enemy of the natural world, can prove to be an ally instead when used with creativity and care.

Even space technology—the ultimate example of mankind's mechanical mastery of nature—is now being utilized in DU's efforts to conserve wetlands for wildlife. In 1985, DU became one of the first "operational users" of NASA's new Landsat 5 thematic-mapping system, which yields satellite images of Earth so detailed that biologists can use them not only to measure the quality of wetlands as they now exist, but to determine the value they might offer if scientifically enhanced.

DU plans to complete a satellite inventory of wetlands in the prairie states and provinces by 1990. No such inventory as yet exists. Like the crews that paint the Golden Gate Bridge, DU's Landsat people will start a new inventory of the area as soon as the old one is completed. "With man and weather continually altering the marshes and with hundreds of thousands of acres being drained each year, we need to repeatedly monitor the wetlands," says Greg Koeln, who directs the satellite inventory.

DU's ongoing satellite inventory will help biologists develop a priority list of wetlands to conserve and enhance by revealing the location of unconserved wetlands and the potential they offer to wildlife. The inventory is also expected to reveal regional trends in land-management practices; this will help wildlife managers predict which wetlands are in most imminent danger of being drained or altered.

As pioneers in a relatively new and frugally funded field, wildlife managers have seldom had an opportunity to work with the latest in technological wizardry. Not even the U.S. Fish and Wildlife Service – the largest public wildlife agency in the world – has ever attempted a satellite inventory along the lines of DU's wetlands survey. Indeed, with its marshland conservation efforts, which have already saved some four million acres of habitat, DU has undertaken what it calls a "government-sized" job – a job that many thought was too big for a private conservation organization to handle. Too big, in fact, for anything less than a tax-supported federal government agency. When it first took up the challenge 50 years ago, DU's sole aim was to save nesting marshes for wild ducks and geese. It soon became apparent that the wetland projects were benefiting hundreds of other wildlife species as well. And today, scientists are at last beginning to take stock of the tremendous value of marshes, swamps, bogs and the like to human life.

"The only limit to our use of these wetland systems is our imagination," says B.C. Wolverton, whose own imagination extends far into the future of manned space travel. On a wall in his office hangs a framed picture of a space station. A space station whose water and oxygen supply systems are being developed in an ordinary looking greenhouse at the National Space Technology Laboratories.

Stand for just a moment or two in a southern Mississippi greenhouse on a sunny day in August and you will gain a profound and absolute understanding of the old saying "Hotter than the hinges of hell."

Here in Wolverton's greenhouse laboratory, a plastic container full of sewage drains into a coiled plastic hose filled with plants. It takes one day, Wolverton says, for this wetland-in-a-tube to purify a day's worth of wastewater from three people. What he actually means is that it would take one day for this filter to clean a day's worth of waste from three *astronauts*. Wolverton's greatest professional aspiration is to have his research lead one day to a virtually self-sufficient space station in which humans and plants live interdependently in a "closed ecological life-support system." Supply ships would not have to constantly shuttle back and forth to such a station with food, water and oxygen tanks from earth. In a perpetual cycle of life, a plant filter system would convert wastewater back into drinking water; the plants also would absorb pollution from the air and provide food and oxygen to the space travelers. Through their own bodily functions, the humans, in turn, would provide moisture, fertilizer and carbon dioxide to the plants.

Maybe that image comes closest to capsulizing the value of wetlands. After all, how important must wetlands be if they can provide everything we need to survive? And how valuable must they be if they become the first natural environment that we take with us to other worlds?

Up on the Farm

By George Stanley

Four of us sit in Charlie Piekarski's kitchen, eating cookies and drinking lemonade on a broiling summer day. "You know," Charlie says, "the smaller wetlands, the ones the size of this house, the kind people called nuisance potholes? They were important to a lot of ducks."

There's something strange about the way Charlie is talking – about the way he and his brother John have been talking throughout the afternoon. The two farmers keep referring to ducks and wetlands in the past tense.

"We've seen the ducks as they were," John says. "It was really fun to watch."

It's as if Charlie's kitchen has been transported to the future and we are sitting at the table – Charlie, John, wildlife biologist Carl Madsen and I – harking back to the days when there were ducks.

Not all of western Minnesota's waterfowl and wetlands have disappeared, of course. But there are much fewer of each around than when Charlie and John, both in their late thirties, were growing up. One survey revealed that 40 percent of the potholes that existed in this area in 1964 were drained by 1974. A more recent study estimates that 90 percent of Minnesota's historical wetland acreage has been destroyed.

The numbers are similar on a national scale. The federal government estimates that less than 95 million wetland acres remain of the 215 million "original" acres believed to exist in 1776 within the present boundaries of the United States. And the destruction continues. Every year this country loses roughly half-a-million more acres of marsh.

Many people view a marsh on their land much as they would an unimproved basement in their house. Finish the basement and you add value and living space to your home; finish off the marsh and you add value and operating space to your property. It's often less expensive and more convenient to drain flooded acres than to buy additional property, and in most cases a drained wetland basin can be used like any dry land: as the site of a housing development, a warehouse, a factory; as a fairway at a golf course or runway at an airfield; as a parking lot, a playground or a tiny stretch of interstate highway.

In all likelihood, however, the drained area will be devoted to none of these uses. It will be used to grow more row crops. Agriculture is responsible for nearly 90 percent of the wetland destruction in America.

This is not because farmers are a nasty lot, insensitive to wildlife and the environment. To use two convenient examples, Charlie and John Piekarski are about as friendly and likable as people can be. They love the outdoors, they hunt and fish, they even attend the Ducks Unlimited dinner in Fergus Falls. One of every seven acres that Charlie farms has been set aside under conservation leases and easements. Yet Charlie and John have drained wetlands in the past and can easily imagine conditions that would cause them to drain again.

The Problems

Some farmers drain marshes, as Charlie and John will tell you, simply because it's their nature. "If there's a will or a way and a transit or a bulldozer, they're going to drain," Charlie says. "All their lives they've farmed and they like to grow things. They want to grow something on every acre. It's an urge – like the urge a guy gets to hunt ducks in the fall."

Other farmers drain to make more money. "That's a pretty strong incentive," Charlie says. "Especially now that we're in such a pinch because of interest rates and the high cost of equipment, fertilizer, seed, even land taxes. Everything is high except the price you get for your crops."

VALUE OF A MARSH

There's no doubt that wetland drainage has proven to be profitable, at least in the short term, to many farmers. This is partly because their drainage costs have been subsidized by the federal government – the same government that spends millions in other programs to encourage wetland conservation.

Farmers, for example, can deduct from their federal income taxes the cost of converting wetland to cropland. The risk they take in developing chancy land for agriculture has been further diminished over the years by federal programs that reimburse farmers for crop failures. Farm policy has generally held that once a couple of crops are harvested from a drained wetland, the basin is considered established cropland. From then on, the farmer can collect federal disaster or deficiency payments whenever wet weather floods out this new "field" and drowns a crop. Worse yet, the govern-

ment has often permitted farmers who transform marshes into cropland to receive federal money for leaving that same land idle and unfarmed. Year after year, farmers who converted marshland into cropland were able to *increase* the number of acres that they would be rewarded by the government for *removing* from crop production in "set-aside" programs. The intent of these price-support programs was to idle enough land to reduce crop surpluses so that market prices would rise to a level where farmers could stay in business without massive government support. Instead, the programs did exactly the opposite by encouraging farmers to develop and plant lands that they'd never farmed before. The set-aside programs required a farmer to retire a percentage of his farmland for one year in order to qualify for federal price-support payments. The more acres of established cropland a farmer owned, the more land he was rewarded for *not* farming. As a result, farmers through the seventies and early eighties continued to convert wetlands and woodlands into cropland even as tremendous grain surpluses choked the farm economy and added to the financial woes of the federal government, which guarantees farmers a base price for their grain.

But there is more to this than lost marshes and wasted dollars. When farmers destroy wetlands, the water doesn't simply evaporate away – it flows onto neighboring lands. This prompts the neighbors to dig their own ditches and lay their own drain tiles to rush the water onward. Eventually these waters – laden with silt, herbicides and insecticides – reach a lake or river. The river grows polluted, its game fish die, its level rises. In springtime, unwanted meltwaters don't pool into marshes, but rush off of upstream farms, doing their part to overload the river and flood lands downstream. The inundated downstream farms and towns collect flood-disaster benefits from the government. Millions more are spent by the

Canvasbacks over wheat field

Farmer and his land

Army Corps of Engineers on flood-control projects that convert the raging river into an untroublesome canal and in the process destroy additional sloughs and backwaters.

Over and above all of this, groundwater levels often retreat and decline when wetland water on the surface is whisked away, forcing people to dig deep to tap water supplies once considered unlimited. Soils kept vital by plentiful supplies of surface and groundwater become less productive.

The most immediate and visible impact of wetland destruction is the loss of beauty and diversity that results as an entire community of life trickles down the drain. Perhaps the most fertile places on our planet, wetlands are home to thousands of species of plants, insects, reptiles, birds, amphibians and mammals. Some 40 mammal species and 224 bird species occur on Ducks Unlimited marshes in Canada, where wetland drainage for agriculture keeps pace with that in the United States.

Not surprisingly, the same technologies, government policies and economic systems that have promoted wetland drain-

age have spurred the destruction of other wildlife habitats. Woodlots and fencerows are cleared, just as marshes are drained, to raise the base acreage eligible for price-support programs and to scrape a few extra dollars off the land in a tight economy. Farmers have become specialists, planting and harvesting only one, two or three types of crops with giant machinery that requires lots of open space to maneuver. Herbicides aimed at weeds kill many food and cover plants important to native wildlife species. Insecticides aimed at agricultural pests eliminate the staple foods in many birds' diets.

Fewer and fewer birds, rabbits and other small animals retreat to the tiny plots of cover that remain. Skunks, foxes, raccoons and other midsized predators able to thrive in agricultural settings pick these vestiges of cover virtually clean of prey.

"Agricultural activities have long been recognized as having a major impact on wildlife," writes Ken Cook in *Eroding Eden*, a pamphlet published by the Roosevelt Center for American Policy Studies. "After all, the very essence of agriculture is to reduce biological diversity so that domesticated plants and animals can be produced in greater abundance, relatively free of competition for food, water or sunlight."

Sportsmen with four or five decades behind them and younger people who have listened to their fathers' hunting tales or have read reprints of old sporting literature realize that there was much more game in America 30 or 40 years ago. Many factors have been blamed for the decline: industrial pollution, overpopulation, urban expansion, overshooting, acid rain ... and surely some local wildlife populations have been affected by these forces.

But most of America's people are concentrated in relatively small urban spaces and coal-fueled factories were running

Jackrabbit in fencerow

livestock in addition to crops. We went through a rapid transition in the late 1950s and early 1960s. We began to see consolidation of small fields into larger ones. The amount of land devoted to row crops, mainly corn, tripled in the pheasant range in Minnesota. The area in small grains declined from eight million acres to just about three million acres. Traditional crop rotations of small grains, followed by hay and then by row crops, then back to small grains, virtually have been eliminated. Today, we are looking at row crops and little else."

Very little else. Research conducted on the farmlands of Illinois concluded that "declining harvests of rabbits, quail and pheasants during recent decades were each significantly correlated with increasing acres of row crops."

In a separate Illinois study, researchers investigated how changes in farming practices had affected grassland bird species. The results paint a poignant picture of to what extent wildlife has been affected by modern row-crop agriculture:

Decline of Grassland Birds in Illinois, 1957-1982*

Species	Percentage population loss
Savannah Sparrow	98
Bobolink	97
Dickcissel	96
Grasshopper Sparrow	96
Henslow's Sparrow	94
Upland Sandpiper	92
Meadowlarks (2 species)	84

Source: Graber and Graber, 1983

full bore long before quail grew sparse in Iowa and wild pheasants became rare in Illinois. Only one industry had the capacity to wipe out wildlife from Florida to Quebec, from Texas to Manitoba, from California to British Columbia. Only agriculture could carve a death swath the continent wide.

Dr. Alfred Berner, an expert on farmland wildlife with the Minnesota Department of Natural Resources, explains that: "Back in the forties, we had a lot of small fields in Minnesota with wetlands scattered throughout and quite a bit of acreage devoted to forage crops, because most farmers produced

Why is there less wildlife in America today? Because no room has been left on the farm for pheasants, rabbits, quail or even bobolinks.

Solutions

It is said that hope springs eternal, and far be it from Charlie Piekarski to argue.

"I remember one time when we planted too much barley, 20 some years ago, and left it in the fields," he says. "The ducks came in and you should've heard the roar of their wings. It isn't like that anymore," Charlie shrugs. "But I guess there's no reason why it couldn't be like that again."

Charlie is right. Farmers, conservationists and legislators are finally coming to the same conclusions: America's system of agribusiness is ripe for change—overripe, in fact, for alterations that could benefit wildlife and farmers alike.

Some of these alterations have been made already on the Piekarski farm: three once-drained wetlands have been restored, and a total of 112 acres of cropland have been set aside for wildlife as part of the Mid-Continent Waterfowl Management Project. Carl Madsen, project leader for the U.S. Fish and Wildlife Service, describes the Mid-Continent as a pilot program that "pays farmers to grow ducks."

Madsen is a thoughtful, articulate biologist who knows why our wildlife is dwindling but remains sensitive to the family farmer's point of view. He understands that farmers often have sound economic reasons to convert wildlife habitat into cropland. Unlike some wildlife professionals, he doesn't feel that all we need are laws to prevent wetland drainage by farmers. Instead, he echoes DU's long-standing philosophy of cooperation with farmers.

Ducks Unlimited realizes that farmers can be the birds' worst enemies or the birds' best friends. Wetland projects are designed with both the ducks and the property owner in mind. On the dry western prairies, for example, the average DU project not only provides productive nesting and brood habitat, it also offers a drought-resistant supply of water for livestock, irrigation, even fire control. In addition, DU Canada cooperates with provincial departments of agriculture in an extension program that is advancing new techniques for raising crops and cattle—techniques which offer financial benefits to the landowner as well as ecological benefits to the land.

One such method that is gaining acceptance from prairie farmers is zero-till agriculture. While farmers using traditional methods plow or cultivate after harvest and before planting, zero-till farmers don't cultivate at all – they leave the after-harvest stubble on their fields, then sow the untilled soil with a "drill" that pierces through the stubble and inserts seed and fertilizer at preset depths. The blanket of cover provided by the stubble prevents soil erosion and traps snow; the snow provides welcome moisture in springtime and insulates the soil during winter. This insulation gives Canadian farmers new options to grow economically superior fall-planted crops, such as winter wheat. Zero-till farmers also save a good deal of time and fuel by not cultivating. These savings enable some to manage more acreage and others to switch to less powerful, less expensive machinery. Decaying stubble enriches the topsoil; in time this may enable zero-till farmers to use less fertilizer. Zero-till farming combined with fall planting can dramatically boost duck production. In the stubble from past crops birds build nests that aren't disturbed by plowing or planting. A DU Canada test found one nest per 20 acres and 60 percent success on zero-till fields as opposed to one nest per 136 acres and no success on cultivated fields.

"If we're going to successfully restore wetlands, we'll have to do it in a businesslike manner," Madsen says. "Everyone in society benefits from wetland conservation, but it's the property owner who bears all the cost. That's the way the system's set up."

In the Mid-Continent Project, the Fish and Wildlife Service acquired leases on 5,000 acres of drained wetlands and adjacent nesting territory. The FWS annually pays cooperating farmers an average of $62 per acre in rent. Rental prices equal the average profit the farmers would have received had they rented the lands to their neighbors for farming.

Once all the leases were signed in the summer of 1985, the wetland basins — many of which had been drained since the thirties — were reflooded and surrounding uplands were sown with wildlife food and cover. DU joined the FWS, the Minnesota DNR, the Minnesota Waterfowlers' Association and the Fergus Falls Fish and Game Club to plug ditches, remove drain tiles, build dikes, install water controls and seed native food and cover plants on 187 wetlands in the Mid-Continent Project, including Charlie Piekarski's three sloughs.

As a pilot project, the Fish and Wildlife Service's experi-

ment in renting and restoring drained wetlands has until 1995 to prove itself an effective management tool for use throughout the Mid-Continent Region, which includes prairie Canada, the Dakotas, parts of Minnesota and Wisconsin, and fringe areas in Iowa and Montana.

Since its inception, Madsen has seen the Mid-Continent Project as more than a way to produce several thousand ducks a year in Minnesota. He's seen it as an example of wise land use that could be applied on a national scale to conserve soil, reduce water pollution and restore degraded wildlife habitat.

"Too expensive." Those words have been leveled more than once at the Mid-Continent Project during its development. Renting wetland basins, the critics say, would simply cost too much. Not enough habitat could be restored to make a difference. Madsen admits that if wildlife agencies were forced to pick up the rent by themselves, programs like the Mid-Continent Project would not have a great impact.

However, he argues, what if the rent for these lands were to be paid by the agricultural agencies that have been spending tens of billions of dollars each year to reduce crop production?

"For years, the American taxpayer has been paying to keep land out of production," he says. "Most of that land has been idled through set-aside programs on a year-to-year basis. Because the land was only being retired for one year, the farmer wasn't about to plant grass or trees there. He'd generally just break up the land and leave it fallow. That way it collected moisture and was more productive as farmland the following year. But it offered nothing for wildlife.

"On the other hand, what if we were to coordinate the need to retire farmland with the need for conserving soil and wildlife habitat? We would have the potential to improve the diversity of plant and animal life on every farm participating in price-support programs run by the Agriculture Department. Which is nearly every farm in the nation."

Madsen's hope that similar habitat restoration works be developed on farms and ranches across the country received a boost in late December 1985. Feeling pressure from a farm industry that was languishing, in part, because of overproduction and from a budget deficit that was rising, in part, because of overproduction, Congress passed a farm bill that made conservation a top priority. Signed into law by President Reagan, the Food Security Act of 1985 contains several provisions that have been applauded by conservationists and agricultural groups alike. A "swampbuster" clause, if adequately enforced, will deny federal subsidies and crop-failure payments to farmers who drain wetlands. A similar "sodbuster" clause denies these rewards to farmers who break up highly erodible pasture and rangelands to grow crops.

Most notable of all, the act contains a "conservation reserve" provision that aims to stop farm activity for 10 years on 40 to 45 million acres of erodible cropland. In the voluntary program, farmers will be paid to grow nothing on these lands but a protective blanket of grasses, shrubs and trees. "If adequately funded," says Dale E. Whitesell, executive vice president of Ducks Unlimited, "this act could boost wildlife numbers like no farm program in history, including the 1950s Soil Bank. It could mean 45 million acres of 'new' wildlife habitat replacing relatively barren cultivated fields."

"With one stroke of a pen," Madsen adds, "this new farm act could potentially do more for wildlife than all of our conservation programs combined have been able to accomplish for the past 30 years." With the Department of Agriculture paying the "rent" to set aside millions of acres for a relatively long time, he says, conservation agencies and groups will have the opportunity to work with farmers throughout the United States to restore habitat in a grown-up version of the Mid-Continent Project.

As habitat acreage increases so will wildlife numbers. Grasses, shrubs and trees providing food and cover to wildlife will at the same time hold soil in place. Less silt and chemicals will run off the land into rivers and lakes. With more acres of marshland, flood damages should decline and the government will spend less money putting flood victims back on their feet. With fewer acres in crops, commodity surpluses should decline and the government will spend less money buying excess produce. A strengthened farm economy will be less dependent on federal subsidies. Because farmers will be inclined to set aside their riskiest, most marginal land, they will likely suffer fewer crop failures, and the government will spend less on farm deficiency and disaster payments.

With its new farm program, the government could wind up killing a dozen or more birds with one well-aimed stone. There are several potential economic obstacles to its success, however. For one thing, establishing a conservation reserve may prove more expensive — in the short term — than the current system of retiring acreage one year at a time. As annual budgets are hammered out, a government facing trillion dollar deficits might be unwilling to adequately fund such a program, even if it offers long-range savings.

In addition, if the conservation reserve eliminates crop surpluses, food prices will likely rise a little. To prevent that, Congress could back off from the reserve. "Our government basically has a cheap food policy," says John Piekarski. "They might not admit it, but it's true." The rub is that while tremendous crop surpluses hold down prices in the store, they increase the cost of food to society. Taxpayers end up buying produce they don't need or use through farm-support pro-

VALUE OF A MARSH

grams, but these costs can be more politically acceptable since they're "hidden" in massive government budgets.

Short-term food costs can be legitimately reduced by encouraging "fencerow-to-fencerow" crop production and selling the surplus abroad, and this presents a third threat to the conservation reserve program. The government wouldn't have to support farm prices or set aside cropland if foreign countries, such as the Soviet Union, bought enough American grain to create a demand equal to the supply. While at first glance this would seem the most economical option for the government to pursue, such a farm program could prove obscenely expensive to America over the long haul. "Never listen to farmers who say they're trying to feed the world," says Sid Ransom, one wise old prairie grain farmer. "They're really just out to make a buck. The world population keeps growing – five billion, six billion, eight billion – how far is it going to go? I'm sure there's a limit. We can't feed the world *now*; to gear up to where every possible acre is producing grain for the hungry masses is simply not realistic. If we push our resources to the breaking point, we'll just have a disaster of far greater magnitude in the end. We have to recognize the limitations of our land resources."

I met Sid several years ago while gathering information for a *Ducks Unlimited* magazine story on financially successful, conservation-minded farmers. He told me then how he had bought his farm during the dry and dirty 1930s and had vowed to bequeath a richer piece of land than he had received. He planted shrub rows, trees and flowers and even asked DU to create a marsh that flooded out some of his cropland. Today his house and yard are wreathed with the colors and carols of dozens of different songbird species, including many of the birds that those researchers had such a difficult time finding in Illinois.

As conservative as he is conservation-minded, Sid was careful not to overextend himself as many did during the seventies, when farmers found it all too easy to get money on credit. Farmers borrowed to buy more land at what proved to be inflated prices. They borrowed to buy the tremendously expensive machines of modern agriculture. The system encouraged them to do it.

Times changed. Inflation soared and so did interest rates. The same government that had urged farmers to plant "fencerow to fencerow" to grow grain for shipment to foreign buyers imposed embargoes that helped create today's gross surpluses.

Now, in the mid-eighties, as farmers declare bankruptcy in record numbers, Sid continues to tractor comfortably along. He speaks often to farm and civic groups, urging fellow farmers to conserve wetlands, plant hedgerows, reduce tillage, and grow more crops and forage rich in soil-building nitrogen, such as peas, alfalfa and clover. "Man cannot live by bread alone," he says. "We need forests and lakes and peaceful places."

As Sid likes to point out, there are many hidden costs in agricultural programs that encourage farmers to produce at full capacity for sale to foreign as well as domestic markets. There's the cost, for instance, of using oil-based fertilizers to prop up the productivity of eroding soil. There's the cost of skies void of birds, and landscapes so barren of trees and bushes that jackrabbits can't find room to hide. There's the cost of plodding brown rivers with concrete banks, rivers where carp suck air off the surface to survive, rivers more suited to graffiti than poetry, unless it's poetry the likes of T. S. Eliot's *The Waste Land*, where barges drift on a lifeless river that "sweats oil and tar" while the wind "crosses the brown land unheard."

Pintails

New Definitions

Look up "wasteland" in *Roget's Thesaurus* and you'll find it under the general heading of "Unproductiveness." Right beside it you'll find words which the thesaurus editors felt had similar meanings – including wilderness, wilds, bush and brush.

But perceptions are changing. People are opening their eyes and finding that wild lands, and marshes in particular, may be the most productive places of all.

Perhaps it has to do with Ben Franklin's philosophy that "When the well is dry, we know the worth of water." Whatever the reason, we are only beginning to realize the havoc we wreak by tampering too much with natural mechanisms that we hardly understand. As our knowledge grows, so does our ability to manage the land in a wise and sensible manner.

During the same summer that I visited Charlie Piekarski's farm, a team of bulldozers moved in and crawled across a field that Charlie and his father had been sowing with grain since 1966. The dozers weren't there to bury a pothole; they were being used by Ducks Unlimited and their Minnesota partners to build a dike that would hold runoff water on Charlie's farm and restore to life a long-deceased wetland. Within a few days, the dike was finished and the water began to rise.

It rained all through September. When I called Charlie in October to see how things were going, hundreds of migrating ducks were dabbling in his slough. "I guess you really don't know half of what you're doing," Charlie said. "But you hope that in some small way you can help make things a little better. It's time to bring a balance back to the land – it's out of balance now. That slough is beautiful; it's here to stay; it should never have been drained in the first place. I can just stand down there and watch the ducks dropping in. Boy, is it ever filling up with ducks!"

I noticed a subtle change in the way Charlie was talking about the wetland and its ducks. He was using the present tense.

The Trappers

By George Stanley

The jet rose; the jumble below assembled into a precise grid of city blocks that stretched south past the horizon. Buildings shrank to the size of houses and hotels on a sold-out Monopoly board. The jet was still climbing when the grid of Chicago's streets dissolved into a brown patchwork of after-winter cropland. It was a vast yet unfinished quilt that came unraveled hours later in a sea of spruce looking too dark and deep to be contained within fences and arranged into patterns. Still, something down in that thick expanse of trees hooked the eye like China's Wall does in satellite pictures of Asia. It was an endless power line – thin as string – dividing the forest in two.

Eventually, the jet descended over an open valley of rivers, marshes, meadows and grainfields. It didn't seem right. You should fly to The Pas in a bush plane with a bush pilot – not in a Seven-Something-Seven complete with stewardesses and a complimentary soft drink. Outside on the runway the weather felt mild; the pilot called it zero, which meant 32. Normal for March, the trappers would say. "Why is it," one of them would complain, "that everything written about Canada starts with the line, *It was snowing and 40 below?* I remember two years ago I was trapping at Clearwater Lake. It was the 16th of December, and I was having lunch under a spruce tree and feeling sick because it was pouring rain out on my snowmachine."

The Pas, Manitoba, offers many surprises. Once a remote trading post of the distant north, it now enjoys all the trappings of a rural county seat, including supermarkets, condos, government office buildings, a 100-bed hospital and, towering over all, a paper mill smokestack crowned with blinking lights to ward off pilots.

Few folks in the area still gather their living directly from the land, outside of those who farm a region west of town known as the Carrot River Valley. Some of these Carrot River Valley farmers tried to terminate Ducks Unlimited's 20,000-acre Saskeram Project, which lies just northwest of The Pas, when DU's lease on the marsh expired in 1983. Already tilling thousands of acres of former marshland drained at taxpayer expense, the farmers wanted Saskeram Lake "rehabilitated" as well. Thanks to support from native trappers, area sportsmen and the Manitoba Department of Natural Resources, DU secured a new lease from the province that would keep Saskeram safe until 2003 and potentially longer.

Half of the 44,000 muskrats harvested in 1983-84 from the Saskatchewan River Delta in Manitoba came out of two wetland areas intensively managed by DU: Saskeram Lake and basins in the 35,000-acre Summerberry Complex, located 15 air miles southeast of town. The DU wetlands represent only six percent of the area trapped. But fur no longer provides a primary source of income even for the trappers on these magnificent marshes. Be they full-blooded Cree or Métis descendants of Indians and French trappers, the native people with camps on Saskeram and Summerberry think of the spring muskrat season not as an occupation but a tradition... a hobby ... an opportunity to expose old ways to a new generation ... a difficult but enjoyable means to make some extra money ... or simply a few weeks of peaceful retreat from the pressures of town life.

Many of the men take vacations from their jobs to trap muskrats, as a hunter might take vacation during deer season or a fisherman when the walleye are running.

The ancient enterprise of fur trapping survives in a similar state on the marshes wrapped around the more isolated community of Cumberland House, Saskatchewan. Only 50 air miles west of The Pas, but six hours drive by road, Cumberland House was built on an island in 1774 as a trading post for the Hudson's Bay Company. Some 1,300 people, most of them Métis, now live in the oldest permanent settlement in Saskatchewan, a village still physically separated from the rest of the province by the Saskatchewan River.

Though the river is only of medium width, a bridge has never been built to connect Cumberland House with the mainland. In winter the townspeople drive or walk across the ice; in summer they ride a cable ferry. In spring and fall, when the ice is thin, they sometimes push boats ahead of themselves and shuffle across. If the ice gives, they leap in the boat. Every year, it seems, one or more persons will drown in the river.

Wolf packs still range freely in and out of DU's 350,000-

Muskrat pelts on stretchers

acre Cumberland Marshes Project. Some 30,000 breeding pairs of ducks annually nest in managed wetland units that make up only one-fifth of the project's total area, and birds banded at Cumberland have turned up in 24 states and all four flyways. More moose per acre live in the area than in any other part of Saskatchewan. Even more numerous than the moose are the black bears. On several occasions, Dave Phillips, DU's Cumberland area biologist, has been forced to shoot a troublesome bear. One night he had to blast a slug through his living room window to kill a bear that couldn't be bluffed away from his house with shouts or lights.

Yet even here, in what at first glance appears to be wilderness, an upstream hydroelectric dam has destroyed thousands of acres of marshland, and people are upset about a lack of furbearers to trap, a lack of fish to catch and heavy hunting pressure on the moose. Only a few men still manage to make their living almost entirely off the marshes by trapping, fishing, hunting and guiding. One of these is Big John Carriere.

Trapper John

A powerful man with a friendly round face, John Carriere, at 38, belongs to the youngest generation of Cumberland residents who remember a time when the marsh, and not the government, was the area's primary source of food and income. A Métis who prefers the old way of life to the new, John fishes commercially in the summer; guides hunters in the fall; traps mink, marten, lynx, fox and other "fine" fur in the winter; and traps muskrat in the spring.

Trappers wait until springtime to ambush muskrat houses because winter weather would "freeze out" an opened house and make it useless to the rats. In the first week or two of the muskrat season, the trapper might need an ax to open up the

Setting trap in muskrat house

houses. Later, as the mounds of mud, moss and sticks warm and soften, he can dig the holes with his hands. After opening a hole, the trapper reaches deep into the house and sets his trap by the muskrats' entry to the water. He then fills in the hole he made in the roof of the house. When a muskrat pulls itself up from the water into the house, its feet get caught in the trap. By the time the six-to-eight week season ends, a trapper will hope to have taken about five rats from each house. In recent years, trappers have been getting $4 to $5 apiece for skinned and stretched muskrat hides.

John heads one of the Cumberland area trapping associations, as his father, the late Pierre Carriere, did before him. John also leads a fishermen's association and an outfitters' association. Soft-spoken and humble, he speaks often, with great respect, of his father and grandfather, whom he views as consummate outdoorsmen. John's neighbors talk about him with the same kind of respect.

As a youth, John's grandfather participated in the 1869 Métis rebellion led by Louis Riel against the Canadian government. Lacking the treaty rights of full-blooded Indians, Riel and his followers took over the Red River Settlement at the site of modern-day Winnipeg and declared themselves the legitimate provisional government. This did not settle well with the federal government in Ottawa, which sent out its army to put Riel and his followers in their place. Only 15 years old when Riel's rebellion collapsed, John's grandfather settled in Pinebluff, a village of about 100 Métis, several miles west of Cumberland House. There he remained until his death 85 years later.

In the early 1960s, the provincial utility company constructed a new dam upstream from Pinebluff on the Saskatchewan River at a spot called Squaw Rapids. This dam held back in reservoir the seasonal floodwaters that had sustained

Pinebluff's marshes. As the wildlife they depended upon dwindled, the people of Pinebluff were forced to move to Cumberland House. By the mid-1980s, the Pinebluff marshes that John Carriere remembered trapping as a boy had become dry meadows covered with willow brush. Ducks Unlimited, however, is contemplating the construction of a new system of channels and dikes that would bring many of those Pinebluff marshes back to life.

On a bright, brisk, late-March morning, Dave Phillips and I found John on the Cumberland House side of the Saskatchewan River loading cattails into an old Hudson's Bay Company muskrat baler. He was baling the cattails for scientist G. Lakshman of the Saskatchewan Research Council, who was studying the plants' potential as food for livestock.

John
We're harvesting old cattails now. In July and August they harvest fresh ones. They tell me the green stuff has 21 percent protein and the old stuff 17 percent. Trappers knew how to use

these plants when they lived off the land. I still live off the land – that's why I'm so big. If I depended on the Bay Company, with their prices, I'd be skinny. It would be nice if people learned how to use these plants. Maybe they'd reflood the Carrot River Valley, eh? Turn all that farmland back into marsh? Son-of-a-gun, that would be nice.

They used to bale muskrat skins with this baler here to make them easier to transport. These things could bale a thousand muskrats at a time. They'd make 10 bales and ship them out. The last shipment is marked here on the baler – 10,209 muskrats. My grandfather used to bale them; he worked as a fur buyer for the Hudson's Bay Company. In the thirties and forties they were selling a hundred thousand muskrats out of here. My grandfather would go to the trappers and pick up their muskrats. He never wrote anything down. Later, he'd tell his wife what so-and-so paid him, how much so-and-so owed him; kept it all in his memory. He'd buy 35,000 muskrats using that system. He must've had a brain, boy. He traveled by canoe and dog team, and later on he had to compete with guys who drove boats with motors. My grandfather would run cross-country on the portages and stay ahead of them the whole time. They had motors, so they had to go all the way around, you know.

My grandfather was in the Riel Rebellion. He came here with his mother from Winnipeg when he was 15. He died when he was 100 years old. He hunted, trapped, fished, did fur buying for The Bay. My father worked with my grandfather. When Dad was young, he would run with my grandfather, in front of the dog teams. They'd cover a lot of miles in a day. Grandfather used to deliver mail to Prince Albert – that's a 200-mile run. He'd go by snowshoe in the spring. I can't remember how long it took him, but the lines of the snowshoes would cut his feet.

Dad was a trapper too, of course. A hunter, a fisherman, a guide. He used to have 80 or 90 moose hunters and 80 percent success. He was the only outfitter up here then. Later on, his brothers started, then me and my brothers took over from Dad. When Jim, my uncle, died, his boys took over from him. Last year was not a good one. Because of the lack of water, all the animals went to one small area. That attracted all the hunters to the same place. My hunters only had 50 percent success.

Dad was always thinking about us taking over from him. He tried to manage things so there would be plenty of fur and game for us, because he wanted us to take up trapping and hunting. Then things started to change. He saw what people like the Humane Society were doing and he wanted us to go to school and do something else for a living.

I saw a woman on TV last week. They were taking tourists up north and this woman was lying on the ice talking about the baby seals. She said, "Now I feel like an Eskimo." It looked pretty stupid to me. An Eskimo doesn't lie on the ice for the hell of it; he's looking for food. He's not happy about his way of life – especially when people are trying to destroy it.

It's getting hard. Groups like the Humane Society affect the market. The thing is, if it weren't for trappers and fishermen, they wouldn't even know these animals were there. Now they're looking at the Indian as an animal. It's bad. And they're making a living at it. These people on TV were riding around in helicopters – that takes a lot of money. We're just trying to make a living. What do they want us to do: give up our life and move to the city? We can't compete in the city. And if we all went to the city, what would happen? I was in the city. I went to school for two years in Winnipeg; a Catholic boy's school; Dad paid my way. The city is the worst place a person can go, in my opinion, if you're from the North. But I wish I'd kept going to school. Maybe I would've learned how to deal better with these problems from outside.

It's warm enough now for muskrats; in another two weeks I'll go trapping. I still like to use a dog team when I trap. Dogs are cheaper than Skidoos. A snowmachine uses 10 gallons of gas — that's $25. For a dog, all I need is one muskrat or one fish to feed him. My brother only needs one dog to pull his sled; I need three with my size. I still do some dog racing, though — it's fun. My dogs like it, but I lose. Too heavy.

Winter trapping wasn't much this year, but I did just sell a lynx for $650. My brother got $714 for a cat at an auction. My other brother got $450 for a small cat. But lynx are down. When we were catching lynx, we caught 36, 21, 26. The last two years we didn't catch a damn thing.

This winter I went to a place that hadn't been trapped in 30 years, and I went to the biggest tree to put my trap there and I found a notch where a trap had been set years before. For lynx

Trapper with dog team

you go to the biggest tree or to the tree closest to a point on a riverbank, and you place the trap so that the snow won't hit it much. Or you go to a beaver house. I put up a duck wing in the tree for attraction. For bait I save the guts and heads of the ducks my hunters get in the fall.

Mink used to be the number one animal for winter trapping; used to be you could get 50, 60 mink. Nowadays it's 16, 20. One year my brother and my dad caught 136 mink in November and December. Eight years ago, I caught 56; the following year it began dipping. This year most of the mink was on the north side of our country, on a muskeg lake with open water, which is funny because it's not a muskrat area — it doesn't have cattails or a whole lot of feed. Squirrel are getting it the most this year from mink, marten and fisher. Mice and rabbits and muskrat are all down.

A good trapper watches everything. You think he's looking in front, but actually he's looking sideways and all over. He can see tracks and sign of all sizes that no one from places with streets can see. If he sees mice, he knows he has something. Mink, coyote and other animals can feed on mice instead of muskrats. If there's no sign of mice and no sign of rabbits, he knows he's in bad shape. These are the kinds of things a trapper's always looking for. When people want to find sign, they should send out trappers. But when someone gets lost in the bush, who do they get? A policeman from the city. He can't see sign; he doesn't know the country.

It's like some of these scientists — they tagged eight moose and all eight died. We think the tagging is causing it. The moose goes into the bush to try and rub the damn thing off and the wolf gets him. They've said the wolf only kills the sick, the young and the old, but we're predators and we like big, healthy animals — the wolf likes them too, if he can catch them. I know a trapper up north who was out with a researcher and

Wolf tracks

they saw a wolf chasing a big caribou. When the caribou saw that it was only one wolf, it stood its ground and fought. But the rest of the pack was running along through the bush. When the caribou stopped, the other wolves caught up and came out and killed it. That's what the trapper saw, but it isn't how it came out in the researcher's report.

In the old days, hunters imitated the wolf. You see a pair of tracks close together and that tells you the wolf is going slow. Then you can see where he's crawling up to the moose on his belly – a good hunter will learn from that. Then you can see where they both take off, wolf and moose, and go crashing through the willows. Willows won't stop a wolf.

Three years back we had a lot of wolves. This year the wolves are down, the moose are up. The biologists are saying now that the bear is our biggest problem. Last year the province tried to get more interest in bear hunting by saying anyone with a moose permit could shoot a bear. But when moose season started in September there was snow on the ground and the bears were starting to hibernate, so that didn't do anything.

I know that bear eat muskrat when there's low water. Coyote eat them too. When the water's low, all these predators come to the slough and have a field day. There was one experiment where they looked at 12 bear and found they were eating mostly muskrat and duck eggs. One bear had a dead moose calf in it. The trappers and biologists had seen the calf and all of a sudden it disappeared. They opened up the bear and found its hooves.

Skunks come down to the marsh too. Especially on the warm days – they come looking for eggs, muskrat, mice. We get them in our traps. When I was a little guy, they used skunk oil for medicine. It was the only thing we had to attack whooping cough. An old lady who practiced natural medicine gave us a drop when we were kids. I never got whooping cough, so it

must have worked. It's not the same thing you smell when a skunk lets go, it's just an oil – no worse than cod-liver oil. But that old way of practicing medicine has been destroyed. The medicine woman, or whatever you want to call her, she tried to stay at it, but one day the government fined her $35 and she quit.

The old-timers have a saying when things get rough – they say, "When I was born, my parents shot off a gun and called me a man." I was talking to David Goulet and he said that to me. He's 71 years old, and was coming out of the marsh when his snowmachine went through the ice. He went in over his waders – that's three, four feet of water. But somehow he got himself and his machine out of that marsh.

That's happened to me a few times – where you're coming out of the marsh with dog sleds or Skidoos and go through up to your chest. Three years ago we were trapping when they decided to release water up at Squaw Rapids. All of a sudden water started rising up the banks. We couldn't leave the dogs, so we waited four days watching the ice float by. It got to where there wasn't a hundred yards around our camp that wasn't covered by three, four feet of water and ice. Our food ran out and we had to get food for the dogs. It froze over a little and the water went down some, so me and my brother tried to get out in Skidoos. All of a sudden the ice breaks. It took us half a day to get the Skidoos out of that water. Finally we got them out and we traveled in on the river. I walked in front of the Skidoos to make sure the ice was okay. We got into camp about 10 that night. Our clothes were frozen, our feet were frozen, but the rest of us stayed warm because we were moving around so much.

I remember the old days at Pinebluff. In the spring, when I was a boy, everyone would be in the outcamps during the trapping season. Whole families would be out on the marsh.

There were so many trappers that one group would start to yell, and they'd keep the yell going. And you could hear it carry from marsh to marsh.

There aren't any trappers out there now, though. Only the willows.

Norman Sinclair

While John Carriere rarely spends a day indoors, Norman Sinclair enjoys only a few weeks of each year out on the marsh. In that, he's more typical of the modern trapper than John. A 38-year-old Métis, Norman looks much younger. His face is unlined and there are just a few scattered flecks of gray in his black hair. Norman works as assistant manager of The Pas IGA grocery store and in his spare time he coaches a grade-school soccer team. He took two weeks vacation to trap muskrats on Saskeram Lake.

Norman had his name on a waiting list for two years before he finally received a trapping spot on Saskeram Lake. Using aerial house counts as a guide, the Saskeram Trappers' Council divided the marsh 20 ways this season, allocating roughly 125 muskrat houses to each trapper.

Many people of The Pas who've been around for a few decades have fond memories of Saskeram as a trapper and hunters' paradise. Every spring, local meltwaters would spill over the banks of the Saskatchewan River, rush into Saskeram, then gradually recede. In July, the marsh would receive a second freshwater flushing when a delayed runoff rolled in from the Rocky Mountains, 800 miles to the west. These natural high-water/low-water cycles fostered abundant plant growth, which led in turn to tremendous populations of furbearers, waterfowl and other wildlife. But the dam upstream at Squaw Rapids and a second built downstream at Grand Rapids put an end to the river's cycles. By 1975,

the year before DU conducted a "drawdown" on Saskeram, the entire marsh supported a mere 50 muskrat houses.

In drawing down Saskeram, DU drained the basin for two years, then reflooded it to simulate a drought-flood cycle. In 1978, the first year after reflooding, Saskeram again supported 50 houses. Then the population exploded. Saskeram had 230 houses in 1979, 955 in 1980, and nearly 4,000 houses by 1983. This tremendous increase in rat numbers indicates how DU's methods of marsh management can radically increase – or, in this case, reestablish – a wetland's fertility to the benefit of furbearers as well as waterfowl.

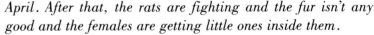

Smoking muskrat meat

métis trappers

Norman had pitched his camp in the snow on the south shore of Saskeram Lake. The campsite featured a borrowed canvas tent owned by DU area manager Clem Jones. On a clothesline strung between a pair of young willow trees hung two dozen muskrat hides, turned inside out, each shiny brown skin pulled tight and thumbtacked to an adjustable wooden stretcher. After a cup of coffee in camp, we drove snowmobiles to a muskrat house that Norman wanted to check. There we stood and talked under a big blue sky on the wide-open, snow-covered marsh.

Norman

There's nothing in this house, so I'll put the trap back. The muskrats aren't in the houses yet, they're tunneled in that tall grass. As it gets warmer and the water rises, they come into the houses. Some of these houses will get steps in them. As the water rises, the muskrats move higher in the house. Then it gets softer and you don't need an ax to open a hole, eh? After I fill in the hole, I cover it with snow and insulate it. Most trappers around here don't do that.

When I get a muskrat, I notch a stick like this. That way I know that I got two today at that house and none at this house. After you take four or five from a house, you think, "That's it. Time to stop." Otherwise you could keep lifting that trap without knowing the house was all done.

I will usually add about a dozen traps a day to my line until I have 100 or so. I have 48 out now. Got 24 muskrats today. We need warmer weather. I only have two weeks, then I'm gone; I'm not here for a long time, I'm here for a good time. Two weeks is enough for me. Most trappers will stay out for the whole season — about a month and a half. Some will leave because they run out of rats; if you lift 50 traps and only get 15 rats, it's time to quit. Last year they trapped until the 24th of April. *After that, the rats are fighting and the fur isn't any good and the females are getting little ones inside them.*

Things really heat up when the water rises. It's harder to get around because you can't use a snowmachine, but you have to check those houses. Sometimes you reset the trap and don't walk from here to there before you hear it close down again. In four hours you can get 250 rats in 50 traps. There's no place else for them to go. I have a hard time believing this, because I've never seen it, but I've been told that in the old days there were times when trappers knelt in front of a house like an Eskimo waiting for a seal and just kept hitting the rats on the head as they came up. It's possible. You really have to work in that last week or two before breakup. A lot of guys wait until the last possible minute to get out of the marsh; they're the ones who get the most muskrats.

Then all the trappers bring their muskrats to the last fur table on the 6th of May to sell to the buyers. After that we have a Trappers' Ball. There's a big dinner and we give out awards like King Trapper to the guy who sold the most fur and Darkest Trapper for the guy who got the blackest tan.

The best year we ever had was 1981, when we got $7 a rat. You were wondering about the benefits of a marsh? That year I

93

trapped 850 in two weeks. You get a good helper and he does the cooking, the stretching, all that – you just keep checking those traps. That year it was worthwhile. If you only get a couple hundred muskrats, it's really not worth it. You know, it's nice to get out here away from city life where you can be your own boss; no telephone, no one screaming at you. But you can't make a living at it.

Trapping's getting to be a hobby. Winter trapping especially. I get out in the country, get some exercise. There's no lynx anymore, no mink. You can only get $35 or $40 for a mink. Two years ago it was $60. The mink and fox farms are bringing the price way down.

It's not like when my grandfather was trapping. They lived off the wild then. But now – with welfare, unemployment and all that – they don't have to. And it's easier to trap now, with snowmachines and everything. My grandfather walked out on snowshoes. He spent his life in the bush.

I learned everything from my grandfather. When we were little ones, we'd help grease his traps. At night, by the fire, he'd tell ghost stories. One night in the summer we were in the boat and it was dark and he decided to hit shore and camp in any old place. He grabbed the tent and went in the bush to set it up. He made our beds for us and we went to sleep. Early the next morning we woke up with him saying, "Come on guys, get up – otherwise the snakes are going to get you!" I looked around and he wasn't joking. There were snakes everywhere. He had put the tent right in a pit full of them. I jumped up so fast! To this day I'm afraid of snakes.

My grandfather knew how to live in the wild. Before I came out to the marsh, a guy in town asked where I was going. I told him I was taking a holiday to go muskrat trapping. "What do you do with their meat?" he asked.

"We eat it," I said. He was surprised. "Did you ever eat beaver?" I asked.

"No."

Beaver's good eating. "Did you ever try porcupine?" I asked.

"No."

All these things that nobody tries anymore. Back when I was in school, we got caught in a storm on Moose Lake and our food was across the lake. We hit shore and my grandfather found a porcupine at the edge of the lake. He threw it in the fire to burn off all the quills. Then he skinned it like you would a muskrat and fried it up. Was it ever good. Just like chicken.

My girlfriend's a city girl, from Winnipeg. I say, "We're going to eat muskrat." She says, "Yuk." She don't even want to eat duck. She don't even want to look at it. Everyone gets their food from the stores. It all grows on farms.

I can understand why the farmers were screaming for this country. I can see for miles and miles. Drain it and look at the land you'd have.

It'd be nice if Ducks Unlimited can bring these marshes back to what they were. It used to be that one trapper would get a thousand muskrats. I wish I had a thousand muskrats right now. I'd be all done.

No, I probably wouldn't be. Sometimes you wonder what you're doing out here – it's dirty and cold. But it gets in your blood and you can't get it out. It's nice out here. Nice and peaceful.

A Hunter Without a Marsh

By Mike Beno

The little charcoal house dressed with happy yellow window frames stands rather inconspicuously on its corner lot. Smoke chuffs from the chimney and the home is buttoned down tight against the swirling December winds that snow scour the streets of Logan, Utah.

Outside the house stand the trappings of a mountain-ranging sportsman: a Jeep CJ for mule deer in the high country; a camper for comfort; a night-black airboat nose-down on its trailer. Those things tell you plenty about Bill Sigler. But the fact that his airboat has not moved off its trailer in three years tells you even more. Today Bill Sigler is a man without a marsh. And that is something he is not used to.

Screaming along the mudflats of the Bear River marshes, a big buzzing fan pushing him 50 miles per hour toward a pound-it-out with Rocky Mountain pintails, that is heaven for Bill Sigler.

Perhaps *inconspicuous* is not so apt a description of Sigler's home as *insignificant*, for the house, its neighborhood and even Logan itself seem that way at first glance. But then so would the Eiffel Tower were you to place it alongside the Wasatch Front, a great north-south wall that forms the bumpy spine of northern Utah.

Tectonics gone wild, the Wasatch means craggy canyons and snow and rough-cut, rocky peaks straining high through the graying mists. To see the ground all shoved and piled up in this way, jagged and sheer, like a thousand brown and white party hats, that is raw stupefaction to a midwestern corn-country flatlander.

Fresh from the farm that his parents ran in Leroy, Illinois, Sigler spent his college days at Iowa State in Ames. When he accepted an assistant professorship at Utah State in 1947, the first trained fisheries biologist in Utah, Dr. Sigler had seen few things taller than a tassel. "At first I was claustrophobic.

All these mountains pressin' in on ya. I wanted to leave but was too broke. By the time I had enough money, I wanted to stay."

Sitting low in his battered but comfortable chair, a thick crop of silver hair shining beneath the single lamp that illuminates his study – a study choking on books – the 77-year-old doctor pulls on his pipe. A career-long academician, semiretired, who can still be seen wandering about the campus on a regular basis; a reserved PhD and author who reads or writes 40 hours per week; a Ducks Unlimited Sponsor; a former newspaper columnist; Bill Sigler is a quiet, polished gentleman. But there is another side. With a weathered face, boxer's nose and a slow, low voice, he has a penchant for hand packing three-inch BB loads, slogging around in duck muck and driving loud, fast boats.

"My airboat will do almost 50 under ideal conditions. You just gallop out and you're set in 30 minutes," he says. "But if you have to bust ice it takes longer. One day, I had an idea." Putting aluminum runners on the bottom of his craft, Sigler fashioned an ersatz iceboat. "That was dumb," he says.

"I'm guessing, but it would get up to 125 or 130 mile an hour in nothing flat. Now I like goin' fast, but that's *scary*. I couldn't get it anywhere near wide open. I could hardly find a sheet of ice long enough. You have no steering. You aim it, give it a kick, it hits 70 or 80, then you cut it off and coast for a mile or more. Then you aim it again. That can make a nervous wreck out of you." Worse yet, Sigler says, there were no brakes. "I ended up 50 yards onshore, and the more I set there and thought about the thing, the less I liked it."

What Sigler likes even less than pushing a boat offshore was the way this year's duck season went.

"They said that the mallards and pintails were down in 1985 but I didn't see enough to have an opinion. The only day

"I hunted was on opening day," Sigler says. To those who know him that is about as rare as a flood here, in the second driest state in the Union. Two years of Utah flood have ruined Sigler's 35-year duck hunting streak on the Bear River marshes – and much, much more.

A Bear of a River

With its head in Utah, the Bear describes a 500-mile loop through Wyoming and Idaho, finally depositing its flow into Great Salt Lake only 90 miles from its source.

In the fall or winter of 1824, William Henry Ashley of the Rocky Mountain Fur Company dispatched one of his best trappers to tail the traveling Bear to it destination. Following orders and the snaky river, Jim Bridger is credited as the first white man to set eyes upon Great Salt Lake. "Hell, we are on the shores of the Pacific!" were reportedly the first words

uttered over the lake as the mountainman spat out a mouthful of brine. Though Bridger's geography was in error by about 600 miles, he had made an important discovery.

A desiccated remnant of pleistocene Lake Bonneville – a giant inland sea that covered most of western Utah – Great Salt Lake is a dead-end sink. A closed system, its waters know only one way out and that is by becoming clouds. Coursing in from the east, three rivers feed the lake: the Bear, 59 percent of the lake's inflow; the Weber, 20 percent; the Jordan, 13 percent. Hauling minerals off the mountains they leave the lake two million tons richer in salts every year. A brine of the hottest brand, Salt Lake is about eight times saltier than the sea in normal years. On average, every 100 pounds of water you pull from the lake will yield 23 pounds of salt. No fish can live in a lake that saline, nor will its water freeze in winter, but recently, carp have been spotted near the surface. Ice now shells it over in winter. Freshwater floods have done strange things to Great Salt Lake.

When the Mormon pioneers arrived in 1847, Brigham Young saw a lake 30 miles across, sitting 4,200 feet above sea level. There he founded Salt Lake City. What Young did not take into account was the possibility of large lake fluctuations in a desert. By 1855 the lake had risen five feet. By 1860 it had fallen back to 4,200. Between 1862 and 1873 it rose almost 12 feet in response to heavy precipitation, reaching its historic high of 4,211.5. Their city threatened, the alarmed Mormons came up with a plan to spill part of the lake west into the desert.

Over the next 31 years the lake fell about 16 feet. By 1963 it had dropped to a historic low of 4,191.35. Many thought the lake was drying up. Businesses and industry and roads and railroads and wildfowl management areas encroached on relicted shores. By 1976 the lake rose 11 feet. Calamity

Sigler in his study

Mountain country pintails

again. Studies were made on the feasibility of reviving Brigham Young's west-desert pumping scheme.

In summer of 1978 the lake surface stood at 4,200–same as when the Mormons arrived 131 years before. In that time the lake fluctuated 20 feet but changed little overall.

A Flood of Problems

It could never have been predicted, but back-to-back years of record precipitation came in the winters of 1983 and 1984. Snows over 800 inches deep dumped on the Wasatch Front to the delight of local skiers. But by spring of 1983, delight had turned to dismay. Saturated soils sent spring runoff cascading into rivers. Engorged in angry torrents, the Bear and its sister rivers loaded the lake.

Churned by storms, the lake rose 10 feet between 1982 and 1984, its fastest rise ever. Working like bees, the residents sandbagged to save low-elevation homes. Houses in the hills were buried beneath crashing mudslides. Highway crews scrambled to raise Interstate 80 by seven feet. The Union Pacific Railroad raised its tracks three times.

The gushing flood has meant catastrophy for wildlife and those who serve it. Beginning work in 1929, the Utah State Division of Wildlife Resources created a system of marsh refuges covering the eastern shore of the lake. With low

dikes, game managers impounded massive sheets of fresh water at the mouths of the Bear, Weber and Jordan. The dikes held fresh water in, allowed marsh plants to root and protected budding ecosystems from the salty lake. But the fresh water that made marshes possible here is exactly what killed them. Filling the lake to overflowing, the fresh mixed with the brine, and a salty soup ran over the dikes.

During the 1960s when the lake retreated it dared man closer. State and federal wildlife managers took the dare. New, *unowned* land became available, and when the biologists went to work, a lush marsh fanned onto the receding lake bed. But the more the biologists followed the lake, the more vulnerable they became. And then the lake changed its mind.

All told, over 300,000 acres of marshes became part of the lake. Land values aside, the state estimates the loss of things like buildings, bridges, roads, fences, sheds and parking lots at $30 million, according to Tim Provan, a 17-year state waterfowl manager. "Those losses can be calculated. What I cannot calculate is the displacement of birds, the value of a duck, the value of a goose or swan, or the value of a hunt day." Three quarters of the half-million ducks that annually hatch along the Wasatch Front have been lost. Canada goose production has been halved.

"Were we shortsighted? I'd say so–based on history," says Provan. "But the state made 50 years worth of duck and goose production that wouldn't have otherwise been there. We just about shut off a duck botulism problem that was running rampant, and we provided habitat for uncounted species."

Federal refuges were equally hard hit. At 64,000 acres, the Bear River Migratory Bird Refuge sat at the delta of the river, probably not far from where Jim Bridger took a drink. A vital freshwater marsh, the federal refuge was called home by

VALUE OF A MARSH

some 200 nesting species of shore and water birds. But the marsh is part of the lake now. Ducks and duck hunters have gone elsewhere.

A grand duck hunting tradition was drowned when the water came to Bear River marsh. The tradition dates to 1888, when Vincent Davis homesteaded the marsh. A springtime market hunter for most of his life, Davis established two duck camps on the south side of Bear River. Crude dorms and work shacks, the camps served as sites for Davis' friends and relatives to pick and pack his daily haul.

At the turn of the century the camps became clubs. In 1901, Davis sold the first site to wealthy shooters from Salt Lake City and Denver who dubbed it "The Bear River Club." In 1902, gunners from Utah christened the second site "Duckville."

At 11,645 acres, The Bear River Club is the largest. Over the years many Ducks Unlimited members have hunted pintails here as the day's first sun climbed and crested the Wasatch Front. Past DU presidents Will J. Reid and Henry G. Schmidt gunned the grounds for many years. Schmidt unexpectedly died there on a summer wetland inspection tour in 1976. Other DU hunters include Chester F. Dolley, former chairman of the board; David Combs, trustee emeritus; Elmer Decker, honorary trustee; and well-known donors Lewis Maytag and Val Browning.

In 1986 the Bear River clubhouse stands imperiled within a ring of dikes. All other buildings on the club grounds have been swallowed. Eight feet of water lays on a marsh that is ordinarily 12 inches deep.

Pitiful Plodding

From the beginning Bill Sigler made it bountifully clear that our December duck hunt would not be hunting as he liked it.

The marsh was gone so his decoys, camper and airboat would have to stay at home. "Might be a mallard or two left on the open creeks," he allowed. "Could be worth a walk."

Though greeted the day before by face-ripping, 74-mile-per-hour winds, I awoke to a tamer weather promise of only "Strong east canyon winds along the Wasatch Front this morning. High of seven degrees." Welcome to Utah.

"You'll need these," said Sigler, handing over a spare pair of photochromatic glasses. "And we should stop for some Sea and Ski." More than one face has been fairly microwaved in the hard, high country sun.

Heading west from Logan into the clear glare of a mountain morning, Sigler and I work our way toward Mendon, at the foot of the Wellsville mountains – rocky, tree-lined, snow-topped funnels. The flatlands below are for cattle and the white-faced herefords browse without looking up. Pickups and horses and wire fences for miles, that is the flat valley floor between the Wasatch and Wellsville mountains. Different from where Sigler grew up but rural all the same.

"My Dad was a typical farmer, he just believed in work

98

Mallards through the trees

"I'd come up from Ames to do a week's work for the university. I'd say 'Otto, I need some fish.' He'd say, 'just relax, take it easy.' Then we'd go out duck hunting for four or five days straight. Out in the marshes shootin' ducks. Just screwin' around when I'm supposed to be working. Near the end of the week I'd be real nervous, but then one morning I'd come out and he'd have 5 or 10 or even 15 people there with a big tank truck. We'd catch 500 or 1,000 fish in two hours — I couldn't have caught that many in a month. Then he'd give me some of his crew to work up the data. Five days I'd hunt, the last two I'd get my data, and I was still coming out way ahead.

"There was another old boy out on the marshes," Sigler smiles. "Pearl Fronk. He lived on Spirit Lake all his life. His wife died and he moved into a damn, dinky, little trailer. He was a little wizened guy, must not have weighed over 110, and he was actual living proof that some people, you can't do anything to hurt their health. He did everything wrong. Almost never sober, he drank the *cheapest* kinda whiskey. I'd catch gar — horrible fish — nobody could eat 'em. Except Pearl. He lived on corn meal, whiskey and fish. He'd get his month's pay, buy 10 pounds of meal and the rest went for whiskey. He was broke but it didn't bother him a bit . . . he was happy.

"I hired him to help us set nets, and he'd be so drunk that he'd fall down on the way to the boat in the morning. First time he did that I told him, 'Pearl, I can't let you go in the boat.' Thought he'd fall out and drown. He said 'Once I get in the boat I'll be alright.' Well, I really, really didn't believe him. But I took a chance thinking that if he did fall in I could drag him out. And you know, he was right. Soon as he got in, he wasn't drunk anymore. In those days your gill nets had leads and corks and they were six feet deep. Real easy to

every day," Sigler says, looking out at blue sky and snow. "His idea of recreation was more work. I remember one day the geese were flying over in waves, just flock after flock. I said 'Why don't I get the shotgun and shoot one of those geese?' He said, 'Ah, don't waste your time with those dumb wild geese. Chickens taste better.'"

It wasn't until 1942, when he was doing doctorate fisheries work on Spirit Lake, Iowa, that Sigler began what turned out to be his lifelong passion. There he learned about ducks and geese and fish and marshes from people who truly knew.

"The Iowa Conservation Department had hired an old boy name of Otto Koch and his crew of 23 commercial fishermen to come in from Moline and clean the rough fish out of Spirit Lake. I had to work around there and you got nowhere without cooperation from Otto," Sigler says. "Now I suspect this old boy had gotten through about the fourth grade, but he knew more about hunting and fishing . . . hell, he knew more fish ecology than I'll ever know. Anyway, he undertook to teach me duck hunting.

A refuge under water

tangle. It took a real talent to put 'em in and take 'em out without fouling 'em. Well, that old boy could do it better than anyone. You couldn't row fast enough that he couldn't set it. He was a fisherman supreme, and believe it or not, I learned more from him than from most of my professors."

Steam is rising from the Little Bear River as we pull off the road near a bridge and pull on hip boots. Stuffing a heavy box of No. 4s in my pocket, I look at the old professor. Three shells for him. Shouldering his vintage 1916 German over/under, Sigler looks at some tracks, probably size 12, punched into the snow along the winding creek. "Looks like somebody's already had the same idea. Birds'll probably be real educated."

We walk down into the ditch and across a field. The snow is knee-deep. Our walk will be work.

Paradise Lost

"The Bear River Refuge is really a beautiful place," says Sigler, talking of a deceased friend in the present tense, "there are all kinds of birds—shorebirds, swans, ducks, geese—almost always something in the air. Barn swallows will occasionally come in the blind with you to feed on midges. I've hunted ducks there since 1947. Now, if I would have been in a badly polluted area, a very unattractive place, and I coulda killed the ducks that I've killed at Bear River, I wouldn't have gone at all.

"It's never boring out there. There is always something to see, things are always happening in the marsh," Sigler says. "You just have to look. Actually, you don't *have to* do anything. You can think about things, daydream, even take a nap if you want to. I've had big flocks land in the decoys while I was asleep. To me, hunting is fun. I remember the old story about Pop Warner and the Carlisle Indians. The Indians were

no ducks today

fantastic football players once they learned the game. But one day it started raining. The Indians walked off the field. Warner said, 'You can't quit, you'll forfeit the game.' The Indians said, 'We play football for fun. It's no fun in the rain.' That's my philosophy on hunting more and more. When it ceases to be fun, I quit. Now, I might not get anything, but it can still be fun.

"There are two philosophies, I think. Some groups who hunt around here keep a record, you know, a *score* of their hunts. I went out with some of those people one day, and headed off to hunt alone. I was so intrigued with watching the birds that I never did load my gun. Just set in the boat all day. I went back and they said 'How'd you do?' I said 'Ah, I decided not to shoot.' They said 'Dammit, you'll ruin our average doing stuff like that.'"

Nowadays Sigler can afford an altruistic attitude on the outdoors but years back it was a little different. He still recalls a young fin clipper moving his wife and two kids from Iowa, starting out on a base salary of $3,200. Those were the days when the marsh meant meat.

"I was making a lousy salary and putting a lot of money into lumber to better than double the size of my house. You think it's small now...

"I hired some students to help me and paid 'em what little I could. They were hard up and hungry too, and I think part of the reason they worked was really for a few hot meals. We ate jackrabbits. I was trying to stretch the meat, and for a lot of years our family leaned pretty heavily on rabbits and deer and ducks and geese."

Having parlayed his assistant professorship into a position as head of the Department of Wildlife Resources at Utah State, a post he held from 1950 to 1974, Sigler knows the ecological benefits of a marsh better than most. He understands that marshes modify climates, warming winters and cooling summers. He knows that if you run polluted water through two or three miles of marsh it can be purified. He is aware that a marsh creates a well-oxygenated environment. "A marsh is a beautiful thing in and of itself, it provides living space for many animals that would not otherwise be there, but there are other values," Sigler says.

"Over many years I've found that the number one thing a marsh has given me is that it's a place to forget all my problems, and for a little while, have an attitude that is completely restful. One thing I discovered about duck hunting is that after you've been out awhile, it's really hard to figure out what you've been worrying about. You wonder why it seemed so important. Everything is a different perspective out there. You come back with a new lease on life. It is better therapy than a lot of medicines. It's pretty hard not to sleep well after you've been out on the marsh all day with the wind beatin' ya," Sigler says.

"You cannot prove that you were any better off because you went duck hunting. You cannot prove that you would have

had a mental breakdown if you hadn't gone, or that you would have fought with your wife and lost her. Those things are not provable. But I'm firmly convinced that those values are there.

"And if I have gotten nothing else over the years, I sure got a lot of good exercise."

Walk 'Em Up
Breaking ice then hip-booting it across tiny arms of the Little Bear – cold, dark, running rivulets that reach like tendrils through the rangelands, Bill Sigler and I stop for wind. Walking is work when you are too much bulk for the crust to bear and each step becomes a knee-deep adventure. His blue eyes twinkling as brightly as the snow crystals all around, Sigler points toward a thicket. "It's usually open in there – could be some ducks."

"Think so?"

"Part of the time I'm right, part of the time I'm wrong, which translated means, I don't really know," Sigler says. "I've been at this a long time, trouble is, I'm not very good at it. Go ahead and jump it, Mike."

Stuffing gloves in pockets, I grip the cold gun and labor away from Sigler – now 50 yards... now 100. White crust scuffs at the clumsy hip boots and all is silent out here, save for the punch-crunch-punch of your crispy footsteps. Forty yards to the steamy thicket and closing, you stop and look, your breath curling in front of you. You wipe your nose. You look back at Sigler for no real reason and he motions you on.

Two more steps. A sudden, splashing crashing of a vaulting mallard catches you off guard. A snatch of green through the brush and the game is gone, artfully screening you with the tangled, woody spaghetti at creekside.

"Maybe there will be more, Mike," Sigler calls. He trudges

his way farther down the field and takes position. You start working your way along the creek toward him.

Respect

"My first three or four years on Bear River marshes we used a conventional boat, a 16-footer," Sigler says. "You could run it for a ways, but when you got out to the mudflats it was only 6 or 10 inches deep. So you get out, throw all your gear in there, and drag the damn boat a mile or two across it. You hide the boat, put all the stuff out, hunt, then reverse the routine at night. About three years of that and I thought man, something's gotta give. You'd come home and you're so tired you can hardly eat.

"First airboat I ever heard of belonged to the university. There's a question of whether or not I was completely ethical in using it, but I did," Sigler grins. After obtaining a fan-tailed boat of his own, Sigler spent ever more time on the marsh. And learned respect for it.

"I was out alone once, so rule number one was broken right off the bat. I stayed out till quitting time, chased a cripple, then picked up 60 or 80 decoys. I came back in the dark, missed a turn, and ended up in a little pond. By the time I realized I had missed the turn I was stuck in water an inch deep. The moon was coming up by then.

"All the weight on an airboat is in the rear, so when you stick one in the mud you have to get up on the bow to kick the stern up. The throttle is in the center of the boat, and you have the throttle wide open. The idea is that when the boat breaks loose, you get to the side real quick and kick the throttle down as it goes by. That's how it's supposed to work.

"I lost track of how many times the boat ran over me that night. It'd take off all of the sudden, knock me down in the mud, go right over the top of me and stick itself in the cat-

tails again."

Sitting miles away in the camper, Sigler's wife Margaret sweated. Her husband was hours late and she could hear the airboat roaring in the dark. "I finally ran out of gas. And there I was. Margaret had gone into town and called the local airboaters association. Along about midnight here they came – luckily, since I had started to wade in, and that place is booby trapped with sinks and holes and deep spots."

Missing the Marsh

Progressively trailing to a trickle, then only thin white ice, the Little Bear peters out within a mile. The walking was not so bad after all.

Cold wind reddens your face and ears as you snowplow your way 200 yards to where Sigler stands at the edge of the wooded, solid stream. With a camo cap and faded brown brush coat, Sigler looks every bit the dedicated duck hunter. You would never guess that he is a man painfully out of his element.

"Pretty poor," he says, as you approach. "I've hunted here for three years. It's fine on opening day but after that it gets pretty dull. I don't mind if I don't get shooting, if I can only see a few birds when I hunt. Last two times I went out there weren't any birds flying."

For about 40 years, marshes have provided the main source of recreation for Sigler. Marshes have entertained him, relaxed him, awed him and taught him. Marshes have meant sustenance, both physical and mental. And more than anything else, marshes have brought Bill Sigler to know that life with them is a mountainside better than life without them.

ARTIST OF THE YEAR

John Ruthven
Maynard Reece
David A. Maass
Larry Toschik
Leslie C. Kouba
John Cowan
Owen Gromme
Harry Curieux Adamson
Lee LeBlanc
Ralph McDonald
Chet Reneson
Terry Redlin
James H. Killen
Harold Roe
Al Barnes

When DU launched its Artist of the Year program in 1972 even the most enthusiastic of the program's supporters might have doubted that its fund-raising momentum would produce 10 million dollars for wetland work by the organization's fiftieth anniversary in 1987. But the program has proven to be a winner from the outset, and over the years it has generated an additional value that does not necessarily translate into cash. Due in main part to its visibility, the competition has helped spark a keen conservation awareness within the influential wildlife and sporting art consuming public. Purchasers of prints and originals today tend not only to be attuned to what makes for artistic quality. They have, in fact, become more and more actively concerned with the welfare of the wild waterfowl resource which is depicted within frames on their walls.

In her "Artist of the Year" section Managing Editor Nicoletta Barrie has put together a tightly woven tapestry of interviews with 15 winners. In addition to informative discussions regarding what the Artist of the Year program has meant to them, she evoked each artist's feelings for what painting he regards as a "favorite" work from his repertoire to date. In some cases, as Niki discovered, that favorite painting exists within the artist's mind. —RW

John Ruthven

"To begin a print series which supports a project you strongly believe in," says 61-year-old John Ruthven, "then to artistically benefit by the exposure has been very satisfying." *Oak Grove Pintails* is unique not only because the painting kicked off Ducks Unlimited's successful Artist of the Year program in 1972, but because the artist supplied fine English Whatman & Company paper for the print series.

Ruthven acquired the only known supply of the handmade sheets since Whatman closed its doors in the early fifties.

And it is fitting that John James Audubon used this very paper over 100 years ago, for Ruthven has been greatly influenced by the nineteenth century ornithologist and artist and painstakingly follows his techniques. He studies the birds in their natural habitat and uses specimens in the process of painting to be sure every detail is accurate.

Ruthven was born and raised in Cincinnati, Ohio, where he attended the Cincinnati Art Academy and Central Academy of Commercial Art. He now lives in Georgetown, Ohio, where he's fashioned a 165-acre wildlife preserve around his restored eighteenth century home.

After he won the federal duck stamp competition in 1960 for his painting of a redhead pair with brood, Ruthven devoted his talent full-time to wildlife art and conservation. He turned his successful commercial art studio over to his employees and became involved in organizations like the World Wildlife Fund, the Canvasback Society and Ducks Unlimited.

Wildlife Internationale of Georgetown, Ruthven's own studio, is the artist's representative.

Just under 500 signed, limited-edition prints of John Ruthven's opaque watercolor Oak Grove Pintails *were auctioned at DU banquets to raise $102,868. Back in 1972, there were only about 320 fund-raising events across the United States; today, there are nearly 5,000.*

"I love painting eagles, as well as waterfowl, and although I have done many, the painting titled American Bald Eagle *is special because it was commissioned by the Republican National Committee to commemorate our country's bicentennial anniversary. The painting was unveiled at a reception in the East Room of the White House in June 1976 by President Gerald Ford."*

—*John Ruthven*

Maynard Reece

Though he has a lovely home tucked among the trees in Des Moines, Iowa, 66-year-old Maynard Reece may as often as not be found away from home, following the migrating waterfowl that have been the subjects for many of his paintings. He's studied the birds from every continent in the world. In fact, many Reece admirers believe that it is this type of extensive research that has made the artist so precise in depicting the details of each species' anatomy. This accuracy may also have something to do with one of his paintings being selected for the 1985 American Artist Collection Print of the Year or with his unmatched record of designing five federal duck stamps: bufflehead in 1948; gadwall in 1951; a Labrador retriever with mallard in 1959; white-winged scoters in 1969; and cinnamon teal in 1971.

Reece has also completed five federal, six state and seven private conservation stamps and prints as well as 116 print series of his paintings. Somehow he also managed the time to paint the fresh and saltwater fishes of America for *Life* magazine in the fifties. The artist wanted their colors to be as lifelike as possible, and the best way to ensure that, he thought, was to catch each fish. The smaller ones were relatively easy. He caught them, put them in portable aquariums and referred to them as he painted. "But you can't put a 500-pound blue marlin in a portable aquarium," said Reece, so he either painted or made sketches of the larger fish after they were caught. The assignment took about three years.

Reece brought his knowledge of wildlife, attention to detail, and sensitive feelings for colors and moods to his 1973 Artist of the Year painting, *Marshlanders–Mallards*. "I wanted to make a meaningful contribution," he says, "to show my support for DU's goals and to help duck hunters in particular to save and perpetuate this great outdoor heritage." Reece's prints are published by Mill Pond Press of Venice, Florida.

Marshlanders–Mallards depicts a flock of mallards setting in on a midwestern marsh. A signed, limited edition of 600 prints of Maynard Reece's original oil painting were sold through DU banquets to raise $164,400.

110

"Against the Wind *typifies my impression of the power of nature: wind blowing across the water, roughing it up into various planes and colors; the bent weeds, flowing but not breaking; and the canvasbacks knifing their way against the wind with great power and skill.*"

—Maynard Reece

David A. Maass

"I think that if someone really has the desire to go into wild-life painting," says David Maass, "they have to get out in the field. Number one is to know the subject." The athletic 56-year-old hunter practices what he preaches. Since the age of three, he's been exploring nature and drawing. Because his parents were outdoorspeople – his mother, a Minnesota trap shooting champion and his stepfather, manager of the local gun club – it's easy to understand young David's early interest in wildfowl. It is equally understandable how this artist is as likely to become absorbed in the movement of ducks on a marsh as he is to shoot a mallard from his boat blind.

From his hundred-year-old cabin studio in the town of Long Lake, Minnesota, Maass creates paintings which could make any sportsman nostalgic for a fall hunt. Eight hundred officers, trustees, and state and area chairmen of Ducks Unlimited considered that when they voted him 1974 Artist of the Year. "It made me feel pretty good," says Maass, "because they weren't voting for one particular piece, but on what I'd done overall."

Maass' work has received similar honors from the National Wild Turkey Federation, Minnesota Wildlife Heritage Foundation and the National Wildlife Art Show. His work has appeared in each of the ten Birds in Art exhibits at the Leigh Yawkey Woodson Art Museum in Wausau, Wisconsin. He's designed two federal duck stamps – wood ducks in 1974 and canvasbacks in 1982 – nine state stamps and 11 private conservation stamps and prints. For the last 16 years, he's painted the waterfowl for Brown & Bigelow's notable "Wilderness Wings" calendars. Maass' art representative is Wild Wings of Lake City, Minnesota.

Canvasbacks are David Maass' favorite ducks. That's the reason he chose them for the subject of his 1974 Artist of the Year oil painting. King of Ducks—Canvasbacks *raised $171,600 for DU through the sale of 600 signed, limited-edition prints.*

"The background for
Greenhead Country *depicts an*
area of southern Minnesota where
I have opened the duck season for
the last several years. Prints of the
original oil were given to DU
Sponsors in Minnesota in 1984."

—David A. Maass

Larry Toschik

Sixty-four-year-old Larry Toschik grew up surrounded by sporting art from the outdoor calendars, posters, displays and hunting magazines that filled his father's Midwest sporting goods store, and the artwork fired his childhood dreams to someday paint outdoor scenes. He became a commercial illustrator after World War II, and by 1970, he was producing fine wildlife art.

When *The Symphony of Autumn – Canada Geese* was unveiled as the 1976 Artist of the Year painting, it was an "unmatched highlight of my life," says Toschik. "It is a grand opportunity for an artist to take a part of his efforts and have it multiplied manyfold for the excellent purposes of Ducks Unlimited." Shortly after Toschik received this honor, he became involved in another prestigious DU program in which he created original waterfowl designs for 20 silver medallions that were offered to DU members in a limited-edition series. The plaster masters are on exhibit at DU's National Headquarters. He has also created the organization's 1987 duck stamp and print.

Toschik lives in the pine-covered foothills of Arizona's Mogollon Rim near the small hamlet of Pine. He has been a frequent contributor to *Arizona Highways* magazine over the last 20 years, and *A Warm Spot in the Sun* – one of the artist's favorite paintings and the one that appears on the following page – was created for a past issue. A deeply spiritual man, it is not surprising that Toschik credits inspiration as the basis for a successful piece of art. "Without it," he says, "a painting would not have a soul." Toschik's art representatives are Troy's Gallery in Scottsdale, Arizona, and Wild Wings in Lake City, Minnesota.

Larry Toschik created seven designs before he was satisfied with the one he used in his Artist of the Year oil painting. The Symphony of Autumn–Canada Geese raised $226,100 for DU through the sale of 850 signed, limited-edition prints.

118

"Every painting an artist completes is a chip in the total mosaic. A Warm Spot in the Sun comes closest to being my favorite because it is off-trail from the regular course. And even on a bleak, cold day in the heart of a clanging city, a sparrow is a spark of warm life that makes the treadmill bearable."

—Larry Toschik

Leslie C. Kouba

He may be of Czechoslovakian descent, but 69-year-old Les Kouba has a bit of the leprechaun in him too. You can find evidence of it in his Artist of the Year painting. "In my rush to get out to the blind," says Kouba, "I remember the time I forgot to turn my car headlights off and watched from my blind as they grew dimmer with each passing hour." The lights near the building in *Bluebills in Lifting Fog* could be those car lights. This artist has a tendency to hide curiosities like these in his paintings, and if you have shared similar experiences, you'll spot them. According to Kouba, "If these kinds of things haven't happened to you, you haven't hunted ducks."

Kouba paints scenes the way he thinks they should be, but he only paints what he knows. That's been true since the beginning. When he was just 11 years old, little Les sold a painting of white-tailed deer for $8, and although that may not seem like much money today (considering that the artist earns as much as $150,000 for an original oil), back in 1924 it was equal to just about a third of the monthly income from his dad's cattle business.

This entrepreneurial spirit became deeply rooted in Kouba as he grew older. As a teenager he roamed 39 states as a traveling commercial painter, hand-painting highway signs, murals on buildings and the like. As a young man he invented an opaque projector. And as an advertising executive he became so involved with exhibiting wildlife art at his studio that he established American Wildlife Art Galleries.

Kouba won the federal duck stamp contest in 1958 for his Canada geese design and in 1967 for oldsquaws. He has designed 32 private conservation stamps and prints, and won the Minnesota duck stamp contest in 1978. He was named the Minnesota Wildlife Heritage Artist of the Year in 1982 and received the King Charles International Award in 1980. Kouba lives in Minneapolis and represents himself.

"Ducks have been good to me," says Les Kouba. "I want to be good to them." And he has been very good to them through the sale of 950 signed, limited-edition prints of his oil, Bluebills in Lifting Fog, *which enabled DU to raise $305,900.*

"Headin' for the Stubble *portrays the vastness of the province area. The 'big sky' feeling and far distance is shown by the railroad tracks, telephone lines and many fields.*"

—Leslie C. Kouba

John Cowan

Call him Jack or call him John, his name is bound to make you think of early morning Texas duck hunts or sport fishing in a secluded bay on the Gulf Coast. Sixty-five-year-old John Cowan is a sportsman's artist, and he is particularly interested in flight.

That interest began in early childhood dreams, and though an aborted takeoff from a barn hay window at age eight didn't wane his enthusiasm, young Cowan was convinced that he couldn't fly without wings. In high school, he took up model airplanes. He also entered and won his first national art contest, and the prize was a trip on a real flying machine: an American Airlines low-wing, trimotor airplane operating from a grass strip. His fascination with flight continued through a stint with the U.S. Air Corps as an illustrator and glider pilot trainee. Today he flies his own ultralight plane.

It's no wonder that Cowan's Artist of the Year painting, like much of his waterfowl work, depicts birds in slow, low-level flight. "I wanted people to experience what most don't have the chance to see," he says, "the bird's eye view." He paints a variety of wild animals just the way he sees them during the hunt, in their natural habitat. Cowan does not want to be known as a "feather man," and that may be why he's never entered a duck stamp competition.

Nevertheless, he's been asked to design his fair share of stamps: the Gulf Coast Conservation Association stamps for 1983 and 1986, the 1985 Texas nongame turkey stamp, 1985 Texas duck stamp, 1986 Arkansas duck stamp and 1986 Texas saltwater fishing stamp. In addition to these honors, the state of Texas named its Montgomery resident 1977 Artist of the Year, and Trout Unlimited named him its 1982 Artist of the Year.

Cowan is a graduate of Pratt Institute in New York. His art dealer is Meredith Long & Company in Houston.

Autumn Snows and Blues, *John Cowan's Artist of the Year watercolor, raised $393,750 for DU through the sale of 1,125 signed, limited-edition prints. "It gives me a great deal of satisfaction," says Cowan, "that I was able to contribute in some small way to the future welfare of North American waterfowl."*

125

"The Spoilers *has become a symbol of victory to me. It is a portrait of 'the enemies,' the commercial fishermen. Enemies of publicly owned resources, of sound conservation practices and of themselves. In 1973 and 1974, the beef shortage in the U.S. triggered an unprecedented run by Texas commercial fishermen on saltwater finfish. And by 1976, surf and bay fishing had, literally, gone to hell in a handbasket. But that same year a group of Texas sport fishermen and conservationists, liberally sprinkled with DU supporters, founded the Gulf Coast Conservation Association, and milestones in coastal marine conservation legislation followed. The group has subsequently grown tremendously. This painting serves to remind me that if enough people care, something can be done."*

–John Cowan

TO BUBBA WHO ALWAYS NEEDED ONE!

Owen Gromme

Owen Gromme is a living legend. At 90 years of age, he is probably the best-known and most respected wildlife artist in North America. He's received just about every art award and honor possible during the course of his career which began humbly as a museum taxidermist in the twenties.

Gromme's tenure with the Milwaukee Public Museum in Wisconsin spanned 43 years until he retired as curator of birds and mammals in 1965. He did not, however, retire from painting. On the contrary, Gromme's art and his popularity were in full bloom.

The Marshall & Ilsley Bank in Milwaukee took notice, and they commissioned Gromme to paint "everything I'd always wanted to paint." The result: 43 originals which hang in the bank's permanent collection. Wildlife art collectors noticed too. Gromme prints are gobbled up almost as quickly as they come off the press. "My one great satisfaction," says the dynamic artist, "is giving pleasure to great numbers of people."

The dean of wildlife art had no formal art training; indeed, he never finished high school. Yet the strength of his God-given talent, coupled with his varied life experiences – as a naturalist, conservationist, author, soldier, taxidermist, photographer and big game and bird hunter ("I was a hunter before I was anything else") – have created the artist he is today. It's no wonder that back in 1978, when a fan asked how long it took him to complete his Artist of the Year painting, Gromme replied, quite simply, "All my life."

Gromme and his wife Anne live near Portage, Wisconsin. Wild Wings of Lake City, Minnesota, and Stanton and Lee of Madison, Wisconsin, are publishers of his work.

The 1,250 signed, limited-edition prints from Owen Gromme's oil painting Fall Kaleidoscope–Wood Ducks *raised $466,250 for DU. "I feel that the ever-increasing destruction of our wetlands is a threat to human existence," says Gromme. "The tremendous effort by DU to save our wetlands by promoting their preservation through art is not only important to the artist, but to all mankind."*

129

O.J.GROMME.'69.

130

"Whistling Swans *holds fond memories for me of these beautiful birds as I have seen them . . . in large numbers, particularly in spring, on Lake Winnebago near Fond du Lac, Wisconsin."*

—Owen Gromme

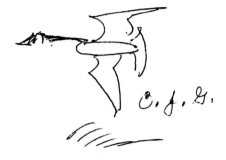

Harry Curieux Adamson

He's had no formal art training and he doesn't hunt. With that in mind, it seems unlikely that 69-year-old Harry Curieux Adamson would become the successful wildlife artist he is today. Adamson credits Paul Fair—an artist, sculptor, photographer and taxidermist who served as his mentor for four years—with helping him set his sights. "He taught me to look at waterfowl art as a way of life," says Adamson, "and that, together with my wife Betty's help and encouragement, gave me the opportunity to improve."

It's no surprise that Adamson chose to paint waterfowl specifically since he's been fascinated with birds most of his life. As a bird-watcher, he's logged 1,854 species (more than 90 of them wild ducks and geese) in his worldwide travels—travels that have taken him to places like New Zealand to observe the rare blue duck and the Amazon Basin in Brazil for Orinoco geese. The results are dramatically documented in his colorful paintings.

More often than not, though, the inspiration for Adamson's paintings comes from the marshes found in the Sacramento Valley, near his home in Lafayette, California. And it's in these paintings that Adamson is able to create the same mood that waterfowlers experience when they are out on the marsh—the mood that makes his work so popular with Ducks Unlimited members. "I paint what American hunters like," he says.

Adamson's work was shown at the first major bird art exhibit at the Smithsonian Institute, at all ten Birds in Art exhibits at the Leigh Yawkey Woodson Art Museum in Wausau, Wisconsin, and at the Inaugural Exhibition of the Society for Wildlife Art for the Nation in London. He was named Featured Artist at the 1985 National Wildlife Art Show. His art representative is Wild Wings of Lake City, Minnesota.

Wild Heritage—Wigeons, *Harry Adamson's 1979 Artist of the Year oil painting, raised $598,400 in revenue for DU through the sale of 1,600 signed, limited-edition prints.*

"Autumn Reverie—Pintails, a new oil, is one of my best water-fowl paintings to date. Paintings of stone and Dall sheep, a gyrfal-con oil and one of California con-dors are all special to me, but I cannot truthfully name any one as my favorite. Perhaps it is because we artists are always looking down the road and hoping the next one will be better."

—Harry Curieux Adamson

Lee LeBlanc

When Lee LeBlanc completed his art studies at the Frank Wiggins Trade School and the Chuinnard and Jepson art institutes in Los Angeles, he entered the exciting world of motion pictures as a cartoonist for Walt Disney Studios. Looney Tunes, Twentieth Century Fox and MGM followed. But by the time he reached MGM, LeBlanc was no longer an artist; he was an executive, and he really didn't like it.

It was 1962 when he and his wife Lucille packed their bags and left the glamor and bright lights of Tinsel Town for the solitude of the backwoods near Iron River, Michigan — where they still live today. There, in the Upper Peninsula where he was raised, the artist shed his business suit and picked up his brushes once again.

On his return to the Midwest, LeBlanc didn't jump right into painting wildlife. Since he still had to make a living, he approached Brown & Bigelow to do calendar illustrations, and the firm hired him to create four landscapes a year on a free-lance basis. Five years later, when the company dropped two of his subjects in response to a slackening interest in calendars, the artist had a long talk with his good friend Les Kouba, whose gallery business was going great guns. Kouba convinced LeBlanc to paint wildlife art exclusively. Within a couple years, *Ducks Unlimited* magazine ran its first cover by the artist. These days, over 80 percent of his paintings are done on commission.

In addition to being chosen as Ducks Unlimited's 1980 Artist of the Year, LeBlanc designed the 1973 federal duck stamp of Steller's eiders and the 1981 waterfowl stamps for both Arkansas and South Carolina. He was the Honored Artist at the 1986 Great Lakes Art Festival in Milwaukee, Wisconsin. The 73-year-old artist is represented by Peterson Publishing in Los Angeles.

Autumn Wings—Mallards, *Lee LeBlanc's DU Artist of the Year oil painting of mallards setting in on a windy Wisconsin marsh, raised $752,000 for Ducks Unlimited through the auction of some 2,000 signed, limited-edition prints.*

137

138

"Before I begin a new painting like Obion River Memory, *the anticipation and mental vision are incredibly exciting. I feel that something wonderful is about to happen. But my next painting will be my favorite, and I guess that's the way it always will be."*

—Lee LeBlanc

Ralph McDonald

From his 92-acre farm in Cottontown, Tennessee, 51-year-old Ralph McDonald does just exactly what he's always wanted to do: he paints wildlife. Although no one ever really prevented him from pursuing wildlife art as a career, they didn't exactly encourage him either. "Work with your back instead of a brush," said his family, and even a professor at the Harris Art School tried to dissuade him. But his passion for the outdoors and desire to paint endured beyond graduation from Harris in 1961 and on through the next 11 years while he worked as a professional illustrator.

McDonald used that time to learn the importance of in-depth research, to make contacts and to earn enough money to make him feel secure about finally taking a chance in 1972. *Whitetail and Descending Canvasbacks* was the artist's first commercial wildlife painting, and when it appeared on the cover of Tennessee's Department of Conservation magazine, it prompted hundreds of requests for prints and an offer of $2,500 for the original.

Later that same year, former Tennessee governor Winfield Dunn commissioned the illustrator-turned-wildlife-artist to paint the state's songbird, the mockingbird. Other commissions followed. For ideas, McDonald reached back to childhood memories of long walks in the woods around his grandparents' farm and hunting with his father and two older brothers. It wasn't long before he established his own publishing company, Countryside Studios, and was on his way to becoming a well-known wildlife artist.

In 1979, McDonald was named Wildlife Artist and Sculptor of Tennessee. He designed Deer Unlimited's 1980 stamp and duck stamps for Tennessee in 1986 and Kentucky in 1987. The Bass Research Foundation selected him as its 1984 Artist of the Year and he was named Featured Artist by the National Wildlife Art Show. McDonald represents himself.

Ralph McDonald's signed, limited-edition print series of 2,400 raised $823,200 for DU. The medium he used for his painting of black ducks, Black Magic at Little Lake, *is watercolor gouche.*

142

"Occasionally, something that you experience, however simple it may be, seems to create a deep satisfaction. The magnificence of **My Lab** *working with unquestionable obedience to his master provided me with this inspiration on a windblown day amidst newly harvested corn in Easton, Maryland."*

–Ralph McDonald

Chet Reneson

A common motivation among fine artists is their search for truth. With Chet Reneson the truth comes from deep within his soul. When he composes a painting, he reaches inside for the experiences and inspiration that he relies on for all his work. His paintings are simple, but they say different things to different people; the artist allows the viewer to participate. And if you should feel the sun or the wind or the rain, hear waves crashing or wind blowing, smell the salty sea air or, simply, just feel good, well, that's probably what makes this artist stand apart from so many others. Through his attempt to create an honest painting, he gives it life.

Reneson was raised on a game farm in East Hampton, Connecticut. He began painting at the age of nine and can't remember ever being truly interested in doing anything else. When he attended the Hartford Arts School, just a few miles from the farm, the world of art opened up to him and he set out to learn as much as he could. "I feel comfortable discussing art," says the 52-year-old artist today, "but I'm lost in every other subject."

Reneson's success has been so gradual that he has not even been aware of it. He does notice, however, that there are no "financial wolves" at his door. He's been painting for 43 years now, and the older he gets, the harder he works. He attributes that to knowing there is only so much time.

After being named Ducks Unlimited's Artist of the Year in 1982, Reneson was named 1983 Artist of the Year by both Trout Unlimited and the Atlantic Salmon Federation. In 1986, he received the New York Newspaper Guild Page One award for illustration. Reneson and his wife Penny live in a restored colonial home on five wooded acres near the seaside town of Lyme, Connecticut. He is represented by King Gallery and Crossroads of Sport, both in New York City, Wild Wings in Lake City, Minnesota, and Russell Fink of Lorton, Virginia.

Chet Reneson's 1982 Artist of the Year watercolor, Hunters of the Marsh, *was offered to DU members in a signed, limited-edition print series of 3,000. It raised $837,000 for the ducks.*

"I had been kicking around the idea for Starry Night *for 15 or 20 years, and it was a terrible struggle to finally do it. I kept adding paint on top of paint, and though the piece could easily have become rigid, it didn't. It has surface quality. Each layer shows through. It is direct, stark, brutal and elusive. This painting is the way I want to be remembered."*

—Chet Reneson

Terry Redlin

If you were to ask an art collector what it is about Terry Redlin's paintings that he likes, there's any number of answers you might hear: the composition, the vibrant colors, the accuracy. But more often, he'd probably say something about the way the painting makes him feel, whether it be drama or restlessness or nostalgia . . . or perhaps it is the pure fantasy that Redlin brushes into each piece. In any case, there's a certain warmth that beckons the viewer inside, and once there, there's enough going on to keep him involved.

There is little doubt that Redlin's past experience in design and illustration has influenced his artwork. After graduating from the School of Associated Arts in St. Paul, Minnesota, he took a job as an illustrator and designer of playing cards for Brown & Bigelow. From there, he went into architectural illustration and then to magazine design. For 25 years he worked, hunted as much as possible, took up photography and yearned to paint. Then, finally, he decided on a plan that would minimize his risks and enable him to play out his dream.

That plan involved two years of heavy research which included photographing wildlife in the mornings before work, during his lunch hours, and in the evenings and weekends in and around Minneapolis' wild places. The following year Redlin painted. The result: six originals, six print editions, and his home in Plymouth mortgaged to the hilt. He left his full-time job with the Webb Company and hit the sporting art market with his goods. Within another year he was a true success story. His originals and prints did well and he was approached to design five outdoor magazine covers, including one for *Ducks Unlimited*. More recently, the 44-year-old Redlin has won the 1981 Minnesota duck stamp competition and the 1982 Minnesota trout stamp contest, and his originals and prints are in great demand. His art representative is Hadley House in Plymouth, Minnesota.

Thirty-six hundred signed, limited-edition prints of Terry Redlin's Artists of the Year oil painting, Night Flight, *raised a record $1,785,600 for DU. "The award was the single, most important honor I've ever received," says Redlin.*

149

150

"The Sharing Season *pretty much
sums up how important I feel it
is to give back what we take. To
help wildlife survive winter, the
farmer has placed corn shocks
at the open side of his house. Two
late migrators glide down for a
holiday meal.*"

– Terry Redlin

James H. Killen

From the treetop studio on the third floor of the home Jim Killen and his wife Karen built in Owatonna, Minnesota, the 52-year-old artist looks out over the 60 acres of land that make up his very own private wildlife preserve. You couldn't find a more contented man. He's healthy, happy, crazy about his children and doing something he loves – painting.

But it hasn't always been so easy. In earlier years Killen felt pulled in a number of different directions. He started out in forestry at Mankato State, but graduated with a major in art and minor in psychology. He served as assistant to a clinical psychologist during his stint in the army, and later accepted a fellowship at the University of Minnesota to study for his master's in that field. His interest in art persisted, however, and he left school after only a few months to work as a design artist for Josten's – a jewelry and yearbook manufacturer.

Over time, Killen disciplined himself to paint every evening. He began showing his watercolors on the art fair circuit. He changed his subject matter from Americana to wildlife to a combination of wildlife and Americana – using a rustic barn or an old piece of farm machinery that would remind people of earlier, less complicated days. He developed a style that was fresh and different, and as soon as he was confident with it, he ventured out on his own.

What followed was a wide array of awards and honors including the 1980 Minnesota Conservation Leadership Award, duck stamps from South Carolina in 1983 and North Carolina and Pennsylvania in 1984, and the 1985 Minnesota pheasant stamp. He was named Artist of the Year by the Minnesota Wildlife Heritage Foundation in 1983 and the National Wildlife Art Show named him its 1983 Featured Artist. Killen is represented by Wild Wings in Lake City, Minnesota, and Voyageur Art in Minneapolis.

That Special Time, *Jim Killen's Artist of the Year watercolor, raised $1,246,000 for DU through the sale of 4,450 signed, limited-edition prints.*

153

"The Geese of Squaw Creek
represents the really good hunts
I have enjoyed with my friends
and family. This area along the
Missouri River is an exciting
place to hunt. There are always
birds working the river or fields,
and whether you fill out or not,
you know you've been hunting."

—James H. Killen

PINTAIL
J. KILLEN 1985

Harold Roe

Harold Roe's interest in waterfowl began in an unusual way. Though he had hunted big game and upland birds for years, it wasn't until the fall of 1972 – when his brother enticed him into a waterfowl hunt – that Roe even thought much about ducks and geese. He went, excited by the thought of a new adventure, but with his dad's warning ringing in his ears: "People who hunt ducks will do most anything."

That misgiving was quietly laid to rest as he watched Canada geese from his blind on Mosquito Creek Reservoir in Ohio. Only then did he come to understand the beauty that motivated waterfowlers to rise at 5 a.m. to go out in rainy, raw weather, and he decided to try and paint some of those scenes that kept calling him back. The Canada geese he saw on his original hunt were the subjects of his first waterfowl painting. "I like birds," says Roe. "I see in them a vitality few of God's creatures possess and I want to attempt to capture that spirit. That's reason enough to paint."

For the last 14 years, the 56-year-old Roe has successfully integrated his wildlife painting with his profession as an architect. He has no plans to leave one for the other because he enjoys them both. "I love my full-time work," he says, "and it gives me the freedom to paint for painting's sake."

Roe won Ducks Unlimited's first judged contest for the title of Artist of the Year. Up until 1985, an artist was selected by a vote of DU volunteer leaders to do a painting. But with Roe, five independent judges chose his painting of hooded mergansers. "That experience," he says, "has been one of the most rewarding of my life." The Sylvania, Ohio, resident has also received DU's Ohio Art Award, and he designed the 1984 Ohio duck stamp. He graduated from Ohio State cum laude in 1953. Roe's art representative is Woodhaven Publishing in Toledo.

Harold Roe's opaque watercolor, Secluded Waters, *was selected over 160 other entries to be the 1985 DU Artist of the Year painting. The signed, limited-edition print series of 5,000 is expected to raise over $1 million for our waterfowl resource.*

157

158

"My brother and I were fishing on a lake in northern Ontario when we saw these loons. The beauty of the large lake surrounded by fairly steep granite cliffs, the protective maneuvers of the adult birds and charm of the young all combined to make me want to capture this experience. I chose to do Common Loon as a vignette so the viewers could place themselves into their own experience."

–Harold Roe

Al Barnes

It seems fitting that you can smell the sea air from Al Barnes' home in Rockport, Texas, on the Gulf Coast. Water is the focal point in most of his paintings, and he can't imagine living anywhere but on the sea. "I like to sail, fish, hunt, sketch and do anything on the water," he says. "Water is *the* binding factor. Everything else works around it."

Barnes is 49 years old and has hunted all his life. When he sits down to work, usually very early in the morning, he depends on his experiences to assist him. He knows from observation, for instance, that a certain type of wind causes a water action and a certain movement of clouds. It is this kind of firsthand knowledge that becomes so much a part of his finished paintings. "You've got to go out," he says, "and get your feet muddy, and get wet, cold, hot and sweaty before you can encompass the whole feeling in a painting. If you can paint the landscape of a certain area accurately, you've done a good job." Barnes, in fact, thinks of himself as a landscape painter who sometimes puts in birds rather than a bird painter who puts in landscapes. "But," he admits, "without birds, my canvases would look awful bare."

Barnes allows himself to paint what he feels most enthusiastic about. In hunting season, for example, he might get excited about snow geese. "But if I'm in my studio and it's 85 degrees outside," he says, "it's hard to think about ducks and cold weather. More likely I'll be thinking about sailing in the Bahamas, so that's what I'll paint."

Barnes is a graduate of the University of Texas. He was DU artist for the Houston chapter in 1983 and Corpus Christi in 1984, and DU's Sportsman of the Year in Rockport in 1985. He designed the 1987 Texas saltwater fishing stamp and the 1985 Gulf Coast Conservation Association stamp and print, and he's won two awards from the Texas Watercolor Society. His art dealer is Meredith Long & Company in Houston.

Al Barnes' oil painting of snow geese was selected from 150 entries in the second DU competition for the title of Artist of the Year. A signed, limited-edition of 5,000 prints of Early Snows *has been produced for fund-raising events held throughout the United States.*

161

"I feel that Three at Dusk *has the right gathering of subject and landscape working with color and mood. Things just seemed to come together for me, both artistically and mentally, in this piece. At times artists surprise themselves. It's a great feeling to occasionally sit back from a painting and say, 'You know what, Al, that's not a bad piece of work.'"*

—Al Barnes

BEYOND BIG GRASS

By James Dudas

Wildlife managers are trying to raise game in the wild by manipulating its environment, and thus to convert hunting from exploitation to cropping. If the conversion takes place, how will it affect cultural values? It must be admitted that the split-rail flavor and free-for-all exploitation are historically associated. Cropping or management does offer a substitute, which to me has at least equal value: wild husbandry. The experience of managing land for wildlife crops has the same value as any other form of farming; it is a reminder of the man/earth relation. Perhaps the salvation of cultural value lies in seizing the offensive. I, for one, believe that the time is ripe. Sportsmen can determine for themselves the shape of things to come.

Aldo Leopold
A Sand County Almanac, 1949

The journey from Big Grass will never be completed. Wetlands and their resources will continue to change, sometimes in ways that can't be predicted or controlled. But as trappers, farmers, scientists and hunters have recounted in these pages, man's contribution to the direction and speed of that evolution will remain significant. We know what it takes to harvest a bushel of grain and a bag limit of ducks. The formula awaits only an "X" value equal to the financial commitment hunters are willing to put into habitat, because habitat will determine the future of waterfowl as spectacle and sport. This principle is neither new nor profound. But nine of North America's most knowledgeable waterfowl managers know of no other way to put it.

"We've got to stabilize the habitat base if we are going to continue to have sizable populations of waterfowl and reasonable opportunities for hunting," says Dr. John Rogers, who has been a waterfowl biologist with the U.S. Fish and Wildlife Service for 22 years. "Somehow or other we must stem the tremendous losses of habitat that are still occurring. And we are going to see a need for more intensive management of waterfowl areas, both in urban and rural situations."

But isn't that what Ducks Unlimited has been doing all these years, stabilizing the habitat base? "If DU had done nothing but create a great public awareness of the importance of waterfowl, its accomplishment would be significant," says Rogers. "But, of course, DU has done much more." Indeed, in Canada, DU has reserved 3.7 million acres and developed 1.9 million acres. It has reserved 200,000 acres and developed 79,000 acres in Mexico. Its U.S. programs, just two years off the ground, have resulted in another 140,000 reserved. Is it enough? Dale Whitesell, executive vice president of DU, thinks not. "Never can be a discouraging notion," says Whitesell, "so I don't normally like to throw it in people's faces. But the fact is, wetlands and the waterfowl resource are like a well-built house. No matter how well-built it is, if you don't constantly maintain it, it's going to deteriorate just through a normal weathering process. If you want a nice house, you are going to have to take care of it, constantly. That's the way it is with conservation."

Whitesell is talking about more than acquisition, he's talking about management. So is Dr. George Burger, general manager of the Max McGraw Wildlife Foundation in Dundee, Illinois, when he refers to the North American Waterfowl Management Plan, which calls for an additional 5.5 million acres of waterfowl habitat over the next 15 years.

"If the goal of 5.5 million acres can be reached, this may be enough to just hold the line," Burger says. "We should be more ambitious, but I suspect that the reality of cost, plus continuing losses of prime areas, may make this acreage goal

the best we can hope for. The ideal would be a maximum effort to preserve all remaining good- to high-quality breed- ing, migration and wintering habitat while it still exists and before costs become even more prohibitive. Plus, there should be a concerted move to manage old and new acquired acres to the hilt." Management is the key word here, Burger notes, because without it, acquisition can be counterproduc- tive. "We should heed the experience of some states that plowed all their funds into land preservation with next to nothing spent on management. In such instances, public sup- port for acquisition declined, because taxpayers/sportsmen saw only a great deal of public land that essentially pro- duced little wildlife."

There are degrees of management, of course, and they vary from the concept of letting nature take its course to produc- tion goals. The idea of so many dollars for so many ducks is still, thank goodness, anathema to most conservationists. But it doesn't mean that we should not make the most of what we have left.

"In the future," says Dr. Bruce Batt, research director of the Delta Waterfowl and Wetlands Research Station in Man- itoba, "ducks are going to come from two kinds of places. One is wherever wetland habitat is left on the prime breeding grounds, which is the prairies, and they are going to come from the big marshes that are managed for production. Within five years, Ducks Unlimited will probably have most of the marshes in Canada of any size that are manageable under control. Ducks Unlimited will be moving into a more inten- sive management phase on those marshes, a factor which will greatly increase their waterfowl production potential." Batt says that potholes may be more productive, but they are hardly cost-effective for wildlife managers, compared to larger marshes.

"I need them [waterfowl] because they are a part of my life and have been since I was a youngster."

–Dr. Bruce Batt
Research Director
Delta Waterfowl and Wetlands
Research Station

One prime example of the intensive management needed to help waterfowl numbers is at Lake Arena, North Dakota. There, DU and the North Dakota Game and Fish Department have increased nesting success in a 100-acre area by simply turning it into an island. Nesting success shot from 10 to 80 percent just by keeping the predators away. Numbers like this are not realistic in most cases. In fact, they might provide a distorted view because they relate to production.

What happens when the birds leave the nest is critical. "You have to view habitat needs in terms of full-year cycles," says Dr. Milton Friend, director of the National Wildlife

Health Laboratory in Madison, Wisconsin. "We have had a tendency over the years to concentrate our efforts – with good reason – on declining breeding habitat. But there are other things to take into account. You have to provide for the bird at all times, on the wintering grounds and on the breeding grounds."

He cautions, however, against expecting too much from the habitat we have. "I think the role of waterfowl density relative to the ability of the land to sustain it has been examined and we don't know what the optimum number is. I firmly believe that you can reach a point of too many [ducks] to the detriment of the species. When you have too many birds relative to habitat, [crop] depredation becomes a problem that results in drainage of land to get rid of birds. You can get too many birds so that they are overcrowded, resulting in a disease problem. I think you can set your population goals too high, depending on the characteristics of the species. You can have problems if you do not address how waterfowl fits into the whole biological and social world."

Hunters and their sport fit somewhere within both these worlds. We are certain of the importance of the sportsman, but the jury is still out over that of the sport.

"The hunter," says Dr. James Patterson of the Canadian Wildlife Service, "has been and will continue to be the foundation of wildlife conservation in North America. Hunters belong to the vested group interested in preserving wildlife." Still, the subject of hunting, particularly as it relates to waterfowl management, is dogged by controversy. Its impact on populations is, at times, hotly disputed.

"The most discouraging thing I've seen," says Burger, "is the U.S. Fish and Wildlife Service and other agencies and groups saying that hunting regulations are *the* management tool. Granted, regulations are one tool of wildlife manage-

"The hunter has been and will continue to be the foundation of wildlife conservation in North America."

—Dr. James Patterson
  Director, Migratory Birds
    Branch
  Canadian Wildlife Service

"There is an increased desire to obtain habitat, and the overall mood is good. If we can get the various wildlife groups together, then I think things will improve."

—Frank Bellrose
  Waterfowl Biologist
  Illinois Natural History Survey

ment, but certainly not the only one, or the prime tool. We must give management to produce waterfowl a higher priority than management of how to harvest them."

Nearly 40 year's experience as a waterfowl biologist in Mississippi and Louisiana causes Richard Yancey to agree. "It would certainly be desirable to eliminate the haggling that has gone on over the past 30 years regarding whether or not we should have one duck more or less in the bag and 10 days more or less in the hunting season. Hunters will remain the backbone of waterfowl conservation, and we need to do everything possible to maintain their numbers as well as the deep personal interest they have for the welfare of waterfowl. There is no other group waiting in the wings and ready to step forward to support the resource."

Says Delta's Batt: "One of the most discouraging things has been that those of us interested in the long-term welfare of the ducks are at odds. There are so few of us actually working in this field that we can't afford to be divided.

Management differences aside, the current low duck populations pose an even bigger problem. "It looks like we are turning the corner," says Batt, "but there's no assurance that we have. If these populations erode much more, I'll be worried about them recovering. At that point, the kinds of professional management differences we've seen in the past will be irrelevant to the sport, because the public will demand that hunting be stopped.

"In terms of the total impact of man on the landscape that insures the continued welfare of ducks, the hunter is still relatively insignificant. But he's the most significant positive force and this is translated up through legislative action and wildlife clubs and everything else. The hunter is still the main actor on the side of doing something for the long-term future of waterfowl."

All of which may beg the question of the actual worth of waterfowl. Do they have any value? "Other than the recreational and aesthetic value of waterfowl, we don't need them," says Batt. "I need them because they are a part of my life and have been since I was a youngster. But, in terms of society, they don't make much difference."

Therein lies reality. Most species of wildlife wouldn't be missed if they were to become extinct. Few Americans include California condors or whooping cranes as part of their life-style. But waterfowl are different, largely because nearly 2½ million Americans, Canadians and Mexicans hunt them. Were they no longer allowed to hunt, the interest of those waterfowlers would drop, maybe not immediately and drastically, but over the long haul, down to virtually nothing.

"There is a way to avoid such a possibility, but it will take more than just hunters," says Canada's Patterson. "Conservationists will have to band together to deal with mega-environmental issues. I'm thinking here of land use and of

"Sportsmen can determine for themselves the shape of things to come."

−Aldo Leopold
  A Sand County Almanac

working with agriculture to reach an equilibrium between agricultural interests and conservation interests. Between economic yields and waterfowl resource yields. I'm convinced we can do things that are of mutual benefit. The job of managing waterfowl for the long haul is bigger than any agency or sector of the country can accomplish alone. The spirit of the private sector has been that it is willing to put up the money to deliver programs. It has taught other agen-

cies, including government agencies, a lot about how to work together to achieve common objectives."

To be sure, Ducks Unlimited has been the private sector leader in waterfowl conservation. Since its beginning, DU has worked with agricultural interests to blunt their effects on waterfowl. At first it was just to provide and control water. But gradually DU's efforts evolved into extension programs that help farmers work more efficiently for the sake of agriculture and waterfowl. And DU is developing the first complete inventory and evaluation of wetlands in North America for use by all groups, public and private, that are interested in conserving wetlands and waterfowl.

Stewart Morrison, who has been executive vice president of Ducks Unlimited Canada for the past 17 years, is a strong believer in the need for what he calls "accommodation between wildlife and agriculture on private lands. More than ever before, I think we have reason to be optimistic. The recent drought has brought home the need to cooperate with

*"Wetlands and the waterfowl re-
source are like a well-built house.
No matter how well-built it is, if
you don't constantly maintain it,
it's going to deteriorate."*

–Dale E. Whitesell
  Executive Vice President
  Ducks Unlimited, Inc.

*"Farmers need water just like
ducks do."*

–Stewart Morrison
  Executive Vice President
  Ducks Unlimited Canada

agriculture because dry weather puts productive soil at risk.
Farmers need water just like ducks do.

"There is a philosophy in Canada now that the user pays
for whatever he uses. Someone who destroys habitat is a user
just like someone who hunts ducks. There needs to be dis-
incentives for destroying habitat as well as incentives for
conserving it. Our success will depend on the user-pay
philosophy."

But will these efforts make a difference? "It can work,"
says Frank Bellrose, whose career as a waterfowl biologist
spans 50 years. "I think the future is really quite bright.
There is an increased desire to obtain habitat, and the overall
mood is good. If we can get the various wildlife groups
together to accomplish the job, then I think things will
improve."

Labor leader turned philosopher Eric Hoffer believed that
the "only way to predict the future is to have power to shape
the future." Waterfowlers comprise the one group with suf-
ficient power and will to shape the future of wetlands conservation. Upon their decisions will rest the fate of North
America's waterfowl.

They can fight for farm bills with the teeth necessary to
prevent the draining of critical wetlands; they can support
the North American Waterfowl Management Plan's call for
more habitat and they can get involved in organizations that
have proven their worth to waterfowl. Or they can do nothing
and expect to lose the precious privileges they now enjoy.

The choice is not new, but it has never been more urgent.

169

DU THROUGH HISTORY

Ducks Unlimited was founded, and for 50 years has been sustained, on one solid principle: that control of water on the wetlands which produce North America's wild ducks and geese is essential to their propagation. By adhering to this singleness of purpose, DU has become the largest wetland conserver in the world. Nearly 4 million acres of wetlands have been saved across North America and beyond. No other group, private or governmental, can make that claim.

Founded by sportsmen in 1937, DU was built on the principle of putting something back. Through drought, nature had exacted a withering toll on waterfowl, and the sportsmen knew that man could not continue to take and take only. The ducks needed a hand; a group was formed to lend it.

With the guidance of Ducks Unlimited biologists the organization's engineers began impounding water on Canada's desiccated prairies in 1938. Manipulating the water in a careful regimen, the biologists are able to manage DU wetland "projects" to the best benefit of wildlife. Marshes so managed have been proven to benefit over 300 wild species.

Today there are 3,000 DU projects and the number is growing by the hundreds each year. Nonprofit, nongovernmental, DU is a membership organization, its conservation projects fully funded through donation. While DU is a half-century old, most of its donation and membership milestones have been achieved in the last 22 years.

Dale E. Whitesell, former chief of the Ohio Division of Wildlife, was hired away from Columbus in 1965. The wildlife biologist was then, and is today, the only executive vice president in Ducks Unlimited's history. Since Whitesell assumed leadership, DU membership has risen from 20,000 to around 600,000. Annual income from those contributors climbed from $752,000 to more than $50 million. And, most importantly, wetland projects that were once counted in the hundreds are now numbered in the thousands.

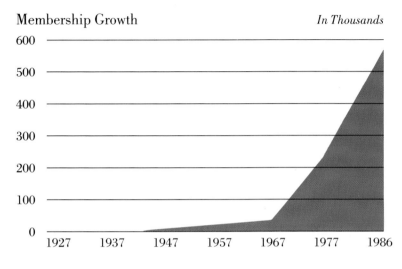

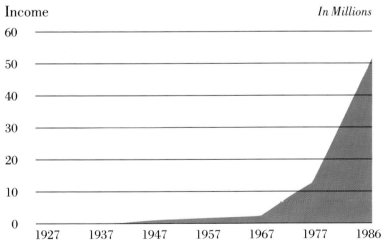

Ducks Unlimited members are the reasons for the organization's unparalleled conservation success. As members increase, so do dollars donated and habitat conserved. In 1938, 6,270 donors generated $90,000 – well short of a $126,500 goal needed to fund the hatchling organization's first-year program. Today, that goal could be reached in one evening's worth of a volunteer fund-raising event. In 1985, 3,700 volunteer DU committees helped raise $46.4 million for waterfowl conservation.

It is a long road from the cozy cabin that stood so smartly at the eastern fringe of Big Grass Marsh in 1938. Stocked with an ample supply of hand tools and a library of bird books, the stout little building symbolized the beginning of a conservation story heretofore untold. Hard work and learning lay ahead. Man would actually work *with* nature instead of against her, in an effort to give something back.

Fifty years and 4 million acres later, Ducks Unlimited has become the largest wetland saver in the world. From Canada to the United States to Mexico to New Zealand, Ducks Unlimited wetland projects benefit man as well as wildlife.

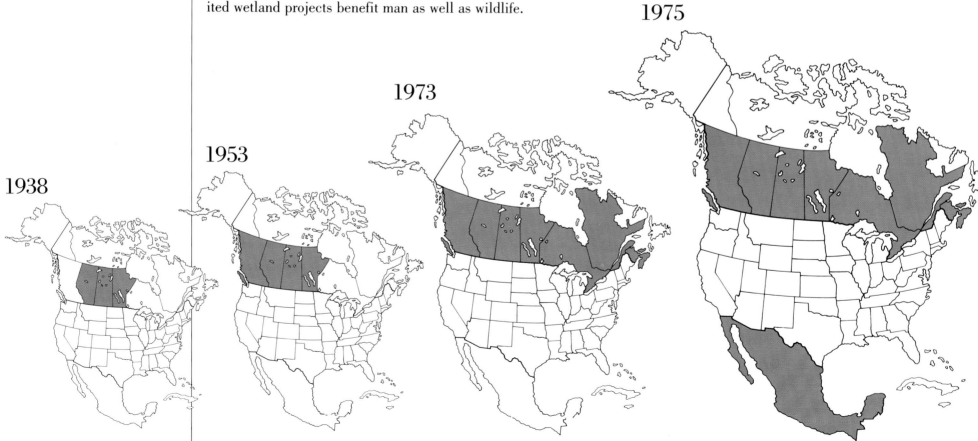

1938

1953

1973

1975

1986

1984

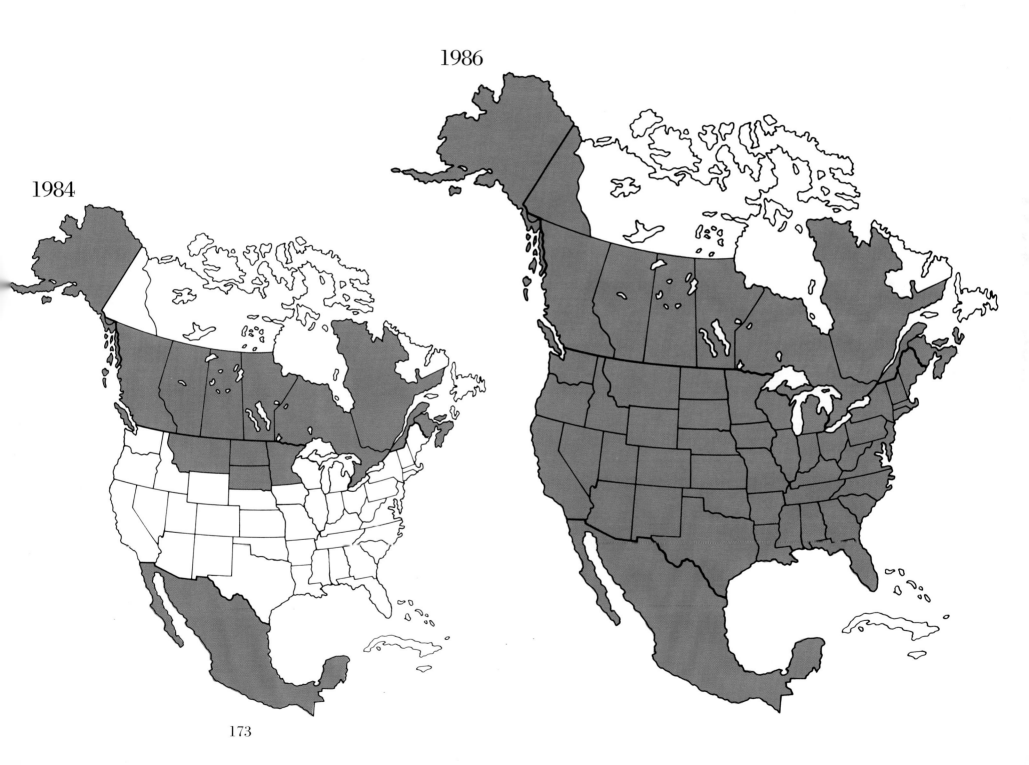

DU THROUGH HISTORY

Joseph P. Knapp's More Game Birds in America Foundation of 1930 is most often seen as the progenitor of Ducks Unlimited.

Formed to investigate the drought that had brought North America's waterfowl population to its knees, More Game Birds undertook the first International Wild Duck Census in 1935. Logging nearly 14,000 air miles in bush-piloted craft, the group concluded that water control on Canada's breeding grounds was critical to the welfare of waterfowl. Ducks Unlimited was founded to do the job in 1937, and by 1940, More Game Birds had turned over all its assets to DU.

Over the years, Ducks Unlimited has been thoroughly tested, has withstood its critics, and has emerged as a global force in conservation – a fitting tribute to the founders who flew so many miles, so long ago.

1929
Drought hits Canada's prairies.

1930
More Game Birds Foundation formed.

1934
First duck stamp issued. Canada's drought peaks.

1935
First International Wild Duck Census.

1936
First organizational meeting of Ducks Unlimited.

1937
DU incorporated in New York, January 29.

1938
DU Canada begins first project: Big Grass Marsh.

1939
First projects planned north of prairies.

1942
Big Grass project attains full supply level. Greatest waterfowl population since 1928.

1944
More ducks reported on prairies than in previous 30 years.

1945
Despite war, DU collects $400,000.

1949
Forty new projects built, best construction year to date.

1951
First Maritime project – Fullerton Marsh, Prince Edward Island.

1955
DU passes $5 million mark for expenditures in Canada. DU Sponsor program started.

1960
DU totals: 568 projects, 975,500 acres.

1962
First Ontario project: Tyendinaga.

1965
DU Headquarters moved from New York to Chicago. Dale E. Whitesell appointed executive vice president.

1966
First million dollar fund-raising year: $1,060,430.

1967
DU totals: 850 projects, 1.5 million acres.

1969
Engineering milestone: over 1 million cubic yards of earth moved. Over $2 million raised.

1970
First DU Mexican organization.

1971
Largest conservation amount alloted to Canada: $2.5 million.

1972
Artist of the Year program started.

1973
DU Greenwing program started.

1974
Ducks Unlimited de Mexico and DU New Zealand formed.

1976
DU passes $50 million income milestone. Work begins on 500,000-acre Cumberland Marshes.

1980
Canada receives 100 millionth dollar from DU. Drought hits prairies – 98.5 percent of DU projects hold water.

1984
DU North American Habitat program begins, with groundbreaking at first U.S. project, Lake Arena, North Dakota. Landsat 5 launched.

1985
Landsat inventories 60 million acres. DU has reserved 3.7 million acres in Canada; 140,000 in the United States. Membership: 580,000; volunteer committees: 3,626. MARSH program started.

A Conservation Chronology

Past Presidents, Ducks Unlimited, Inc.

1937
John A. Hartwell
New York, New York

1938
Louis H. Egan
St. Louis, Missouri

1939
L. H. Barkhausen
Chicago, Illinois

1940
John B. Coleman
San Francisco, California

1941
E. Herrick Low
New York, New York

1942-1943
Will J. Reid
Long Beach, California

1944-1945
A. C. Glassell
Shreveport, Louisiana

1946-1947
Morton W. Smith
Minneapolis, Minnesota

1948
Hon. E. L. McHaney
Little Rock, Arkansas

1949-1950
Harvey L. Sorensen
San Francisco, California

1951-1952
C. A. Gross
Green Bay, Wisconsin

1953-1954
Robert M. Gaylord
Rockford, Illinois

1955-1956
Robert Winthrop
New York, New York

1957-1958
H. Bliss Rucker
San Francisco, California

1959-1960
Carsten Tiedeman
Detroit, Michigan

1961-1962
Stirling S. Adams
New York, New York

1963-1964
Albert B. McKee, Jr.
San Marino, California

1965-1966
Henry G. Schmidt
Cleveland, Ohio

1967-1968
Charles B. Allen
Baltimore, Maryland

1969-1970
William P. Elser
La Jolla, California

1971-1972
Lee C. Howley
Cleveland, Ohio

1973-1974
Herman Taylor, Jr.
Natchitoches, Louisiana

1975-1976
Gaylord Donnelley
Chicago, Illinois

1977
Henry J. Nave
Pinehurst, North Carolina

1978-1979
S. Preston Williams
N. Kansas City, Missouri

1980-1981
Robert D. Marcotte
Omaha, Nebraska

1982-1983
Robert M. Eberhardt
Stockton, California

1984-1985
Peter H. Coors
Golden, Colorado

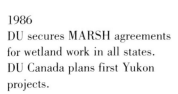

1986
DU secures MARSH agreements
for wetland work in all states.
DU Canada plans first Yukon
projects.

CREDITS

Jacket and page ii: *The Old West Passes,* oil on canvas by Francis Lee Jaques (1887-1969), courtesy of the James Ford Bell Museum of Natural History, University of Minnesota, Minneapolis, Minnesota; **p. vi:** photograph by Ron Sanford; **p. ix:** photograph by Scot Stewart; **p. x:** photograph by Ron Sanford.

RETURN TO BIG GRASS
Pages 2-24, with following exceptions, from Ducks Unlimited, Inc. archive collection; **p. 2:** map by Gary Cox and Mobium Corporation; **p. 6:** photograph by Glenn D. Chambers; **p. 8:** photograph by Mike Beno; **p. 9, left:** photograph courtesy of Irene Foxon; **p. 9, right:** scratchboard by Lee D. Salber; **p. 10, left:** illustration courtesy of The Bettmann Archive Inc.; **p. 17, left:** illustration by Joe Fornelli; **p. 17, right:** photographs (3) by Mike Beno; **page 23, left:** photograph by Glenn D. Chambers; **p. 24, left:** illustration by Gary Cox; **p. 24, right:** detail from engraving by Maynard Reece.

DU COUNTRY
Mountain photographs
Page 26: Brian Hay; **p. 28:** Stephen J. Krasemann (DRK Photo); **p. 29:** Dave Klassen; **p. 30:** Glenn D. Chambers; **p. 31, top:** R. L. Kothenbeutel; **p. 31, left:** Tom and Pat Leeson; **p. 31,** **right:** Scott Nielsen; **p. 32, left:** Jeff Foott; **p. 32, right:** L. G. Hammond; **p. 33, top:** Ken Reynolds; **p. 33, bottom:** Glenn D. Chambers; **p. 34, left:** Thomas D. Mangelsen; **p. 34, right:** Glenn D. Chambers; **p. 35, top:** Stan Osolinski; **p. 35, bottom:** Thomas D. Mangelsen.

Prairie photographs
Page 36: Jim Romo; **p. 38, left:** Richard Wentz; **p. 38, right:** Jim Brandenburg (DRK Photo); **p. 39:** Jack A. Barrie; **p. 40:** Tim Fitzharris; **p. 41, top:** Cal Cuthbert; **p. 41, left:** Thomas D. Mangelsen; **p. 41, right:** Eleanor Brown; **p. 42:** Stan Osolinski; **p. 43, left:** B. T. Aniskowicz; **p. 43, right:** Thomas D. Mangelsen; **p. 44, left:** Rick Andrews; **pps. 44-45:** Jack A. Barrie; **p. 45, right:** R. L. Kothenbeutel; **p. 46, left:** Tom and Pat Leeson; **p. 46, right:** Scott Nielsen; **p. 47, left:** Ken Reynolds; **p. 47, right:** Scot Stewart.

Maritimes photographs
Page 48: Stephen Kirkpatrick; **p. 50:** Gary Meszaros; **p. 51, top:** Wayne Lankinen; **p. 51, left:** Scot Stewart; **p. 51, right:** Stephen Kirkpatrick; **p. 52:** Stephen Kirkpatrick; **p. 53, left (2):** Glenn D. Chambers; **p. 53, right:** Ken Reynolds; **p. 54, left:** Glenn D. Chambers; **p. 54,** **right:** B. T. Aniskowicz; **p. 55:** Thomas D. Mangelsen; **p. 56, top:** Scot Stewart; **p. 56, bottom:** Tim Fitzharris; **p. 57:** Scot Stewart.

Mexico photographs
Page 58: Stephen J. Krasemann (DRK Photo); **p. 60, left:** Wayne Lankinen; **p. 60, right:** Steve Wilson (Entheos); **p. 61:** B. T. Aniskowicz; **p. 62, left:** Matthew B. Connolly; **p. 62, right:** Frank S. Todd; **p. 63, left:** Gary R. Zahm; **p. 63, right:** Tom and Pat Leeson; **p. 64, left:** Thomas D. Mangelsen; **p. 64, right:** Richard Wentz; **p. 65, left:** Tim Fitzharris; **p. 65, right:** Frank S. Todd; **p. 66, left:** Gary Meszaros; **p. 66, right:** Scot Stewart.

ARTISTS OF THE YEAR
Page 104: photograph by Judy Schraishuhn; **p. 105:** from the collection of Win Hawkins; **p. 112:** photograph by Bill Meyer (Wild Wings, Inc.); **p. 113:** from the collection of Keith Russell; **p. 114:** photograph of painting courtesy of Wild Wings, Inc.; **p. 117:** from the collection of Henry P. McIntosh IV; **p. 118:** From the collection of James Silver, photograph of painting courtesy of *Arizona Highways* magazine; **p. 121:** from the collection of Dean L. Leeper; **p.**

125: from the collection of David Wintermann; **p. 126:** from the Houston Museum of Fine Arts collection, photograph of painting courtesy of Texas A & M University Press, *The Texas Gulf Coast,* published 1979; **p. 129:** photograph of painting courtesy of Stanton & Lee Publishers, Inc.; **p. 130:** photograph of painting courtesy of Wild Wings, Inc.; **p. 132:** photograph by Brian Duffy (Focal Point); **p. 133:** from the collection of Mr. and Mrs. George Scott; **p. 134:** photograph of painting courtesy of Brian Duffy (Focal Point); **p. 136:** photograph by Erickson Studios; **p. 137:** from the collection of Ralph Olinde; **p. 140:** photograph by Crutchers Studios; **p. 141:** from the collection of Rex Callicott; **p. 142:** from the collection of Cameron Harris, photograph of painting courtesy of Countryside Studio; **p. 144:** photograph by Penny Reneson; **p. 145:** from the collection of Robert C. Bartleson; **p. 146:** from Chet Reneson's personal collection; **p. 150:** photograph of painting courtesy of Hadley House; **p. 156:** photograph by Scott Hall Photography; **p. 158:** from the collection of Dr. Larry Winegar; **p. 160:** photograph by Nancy Barnes; **p. 162:** photograph of painting courtesy of Meredith Long & Company.

BEYOND BIG GRASS
Photographs—**page 165:** Ron Sanford; **p. 166:** Archie Johnson; **p. 167, left:** Jack Ellis; **p. 167, right:** Jon Farrar; **p. 168, left:** Jack Ellis; **p. 168, right:** Glenn D. Chambers; **p. 169:** Charles Potter.

DU THROUGH HISTORY
Page 170: photograph by Gary R. Zahm; **pps. 171-173:** charts and maps by Gary Cox; **pps. 174-175:** illustration by Gary Cox.